S0-BQW-763

"Andrews and Entwistle deliver an innovative approach to public service efficiency that carefully crafts theory and practice around a multifaceted concept of efficiency. Simplistic ideas of Economic and Pareto efficiency, that have dominated political aspirations for public administration for far too long, are dismantled using a critical and realist approach. This highlights the trade-offs and contradictions that public managers experience in their day-to-day practice. I commend their four faces model to practitioners and students, as it will aid understanding of the challenges managers experience when trying to improve services. Most important of all this books takes us beyond a preoccupation with productive efficiency to reconnect service improvements with democratic and public values."

Philip Haynes, Professor, University of Brighton, UK

"Efficiency is a concept which has widespread use in everyday conversation. Andrews and Entwistle address the fallacy of the everyday understanding of this term by their discussion of the complexities of this concept in this book. This is a nuanced critique of efficiency in the setting of public management, an area of study which is highly contested and which is beset by 'wicked' policy problems. The authors offer a powerful assembly of ideas of efficiency for both serious scholars of, and policy makers in, public management."

Irvine Lapsley, Editor, Financial Accountability & Management, and Director, IPSAR, University of Edinburgh Business School, UK

"The book makes the case for rethinking how to apply public service efficiency in public administration. Compelling arguments are presented for a multi-dimensional approach that covers democratic and economic elements and the interaction between the dimensions."

John Halligan, Professor, University of Canberra, Australia

Public Service Efficiency

The current economic and political climate places ever greater pressure on public organizations to deliver value for money. Focused on this agenda, governments across the world have introduced a series of business like practices 'from performance management to public-private partnership' in a bid to increase the efficiency of public services. However, both the debate about public service efficiency and the policies and practices introduced to advance it, have developed without a coherent account of what efficiency means in this context and how it might best be advanced. In the absence of this debate, governments have tended to focus on the productive dimension of efficiency by minimising the resources devoted to public service delivery. The predominance of this rather narrow definition of the term has tended to polarise opinion either for or against the efficiency agenda. Yet understanding the broader senses of public service efficiency – across four faces including the productive, distributive, dynamic and allocative senses of the term – is crucial to any attempt to reform the state. This book seeks to recover public service efficiency from the relatively narrow terms of recent debates by examining these four faces of efficiency, the relationship between them and the challenges of realising them. A more broadly defined notion of public service efficiency – which does justice to the four faces – should be centre stage in debates about how and why we are governed.

Rhys Andrews is Professor of Public Management at Cardiff University, UK. His primary research interests are in strategic management, social capital, organizational structure and public service performance. He is co-editor of the *International Public Management Journal.*

Tom Entwistle is Reader in Public Policy and Management and director of the Master's in Public Administration at Cardiff University, UK. His primary research interests are in the areas of local governance, central–local relations, public–private partnerships and public service performance.

Routledge Critical Studies in Public Management
Edited by Stephen Osborne

The study and practice of public management has undergone profound changes across the world. Over the last quarter century, we have seen

- increasing criticism of public administration as the over-arching framework for the provision of public services,
- the rise (and critical appraisal) of the 'New Public Management' as an emergent paradigm for the provision of public services,
- the transformation of the 'public sector' into the cross-sectoral provision of public services, and
- the growth of the governance of inter-organizational relationships as an essential element in the provision of public services

In reality these trends have not so much replaced each other as elided or co-existed together – the public policy process has not gone away as a legitimate topic of study, intra-organizational management continues to be essential to the efficient provision of public services, whist the governance of inter-organizational and inter-sectoral relationships is now essential to the effective provision of these services.

Further, whilst the study of public management has been enriched by contribution of a range of insights from the 'mainstream' management literature it has also contributed to this literature in such areas as networks and inter-organizational collaboration, innovation and stakeholder theory.

This series is dedicated to presenting and critiquing this important body of theory and empirical study. It will publish books that both explore and evaluate the emergent and developing nature of public administration, management and governance (in theory and practice) and examine the relationship with and contribution to the over-arching disciplines of management and organizational sociology.

Books in the series will be of interest to academics and researchers in this field, students undertaking advanced studies of it as part of their undergraduate or postgraduate degree and reflective policy makers and practitioners.

1. **Unbundled Government**
   A critical analysis of the global
   trend to agencies, quangos
   and contractualisation
   *Edited by Christopher Pollitt
   and Colin Talbot*

2. **The Study of Public
   Management in Europe
   and the US**
   A Competitive Analysis
   of National Distinctiveness
   Edited by Walter Kickert

Public Service Efficiency
Reframing the debate

Rhys Andrews and **Tom Entwistle**

Routledge
Taylor & Francis Group

LONDON AND NEW YORK

First published 2014
by Routledge
2 Park Square, Milton Park, Abingdon, Oxon OX14 4RN

and by Routledge
711 Third Avenue, New York, NY 10017

Routledge is an imprint of the Taylor & Francis Group, an informa business

© 2014 R. Andrews & T. Entwistle

The right of Rhys Andrews and Tom Entwistle to be identified as author of
this work has been asserted by them in accordance with sections 77 and 78
of the Copyright, Designs and Patents Act 1988.

All rights reserved. No part of this book may be reprinted or reproduced or
utilised in any form or by any electronic, mechanical, or other means, now
known or hereafter invented, including photocopying and recording, or in
any information storage or retrieval system, without permission in writing
from the publishers.

Trademark notice: Product or corporate names may be trademarks or
registered trademarks, and are used only for identification and explanation
without intent to infringe.

British Library Cataloguing in Publication Data
A catalogue record for this book is available from the British Library

Library of Congress Cataloging in Publication Data
Andrews, Rhys.
   Public service efficiency : reframing the debate / Rhys Andrews and
Tom Entwistle.
      pages cm. -- (Routledge critical studies in public management)
   Includes bibliographical references and index.
   1. Civil service. I. Entwistle, Tom. II. Title.
   JF1601.A683 2013
   352.6'6--dc23
               2013021039

ISBN: 978-0-415-50134-7 (hbk)
ISBN: 978-0-203-74915-9 (ebk)

Typeset in Times New Roman
by Taylor & Francis Books

Library
University of Texas
at San Antonio

Contents

Illustrations

Tables

Figures

1 Introduction

The global financial crisis of the early twenty-first century has led to renewed attention being paid to the size and cost of the public sector. Draconian cuts in public expenditure to reduce budget deficits have been imposed in many countries, and questions have been raised about the scale and scope of the state's responsibilities. Central to these debates has been the question of the efficiency of public services, and the ways in which those services might be able to fulfil the same duties as before but with a much-reduced budget. These concerns about public service efficiency are not new. The issue of cost-effectiveness was a prominent theme shaping the growth of the New Public Management (NPM) reforms of the 1980s and 1990s (Aucoin 1990). In fact, even during the boom years of the 'noughties' many governments retained a keen interest in efficiency savings in the public sector, particularly given the large investments in public service improvement that were made during the period (Gershon 2004). Now, in the new era of fiscal austerity, questions about the ways in which public services can be made more cost-effective have become increasingly urgent as governments grapple with large budget deficits and sluggish economic growth.

In this book we aim to offer a more nuanced account of public service efficiency than is typically presented in either policy debates or scholarly work on the topic. Our basic argument is that efficiency in the public sector is not just about maximizing the quantity of production outputs and minimizing the cost of production inputs; it also comprises the quality of production outputs, whether some citizens should receive more or better quality outputs on the grounds of need, whether current output should be reduced to support investment in future service production, and the fit between the types of output produced and the outputs citizens want. In making the argument that there is more than one dimension (or face) of efficiency, we seek to establish that efficiency is a broader and more important concept than is often acknowledged within the contemporary literature on public administration. Moreover, we claim that the multi-faceted nature of efficiency is familiar to practitioners of public management. Indeed, we suggest that one or other of the faces of efficiency we consider is actually at the heart of most policies and managerial strategies for improving public services, and that the management of the tensions between the different dimensions remains one of the most important tasks in democratic public administration.

The idea that efficiency is an important goal for public service organizations is not an especially controversial one. However, in seeking to advance a richer understanding of the concept of public service efficiency we also aim to demonstrate that efficiency is actually a core administrative value for public managers and policy-makers. For many public administration scholars, the notion that efficiency has a place within the lexicon of public service values is anathema to the idea of a democratic public administration; the public values characteristic of public administration in a democracy simply do not include keeping an eye on the bottom line, so to speak. One of our aims in this book is therefore to illustrate the ways in which an expanded conception of efficiency can capture how the daily work of public managers involves decisions about the use of scarce resources that have implications for the public good as a whole.

In developing our arguments within the book, we do not claim that efficiency is either the only or, even, the most important, administrative value within the public sector. Rather we seek to expand and update the concept of public service efficiency for a time in which questions about the cost of the public sector are once again very much to the fore. Although we draw upon economic theories in developing our ideas about the efficiency challenge in the public sector, the book is not written as a text in public economics. Nor, though we draw upon ideas from political theory, is it written as a text in political science. Instead, given the intersection of disciplinary concerns and the practical import of our arguments, we locate our work within the field of public administration, which Hood (1990: 107) describes as 'the study of institutional arrangements for the provision of public services'.

In the following sections of this introductory chapter we set out the conceptual and empirical terrain that is covered in the book and discuss the origins of the concept of public service efficiency within the public administration literature. We reflect on its evolution from being the principle at the heart of scientific public administration to its rejection by democratic theorists of government. We outline why we believe an expanded notion of efficiency can still illuminate some of the big questions in public administration and describe four faces of efficiency that we believe guide the actual conduct of public policy and administration within a democracy. We then summarize the main chapters of the book in which we introduce the public sector efficiency problem, theories and evidence on the four faces of efficiency, and the management of the tensions between each dimension of efficiency within a democratic setting. The book therefore brings together a wide range of ideas about the problems, policies and prospects of public service efficiency, and provides the most thorough reflection to date on how it has been, and should be, pursued.

What is public service efficiency?

The efficiency of the public sector is an issue that is rarely out of news headlines in democratic countries across the world. Calls to reduce government spending, improve the productivity of public officials and make the public sector more business-like have been a popular refrain in the developed world throughout the post-war period (Downs and Larkey 1986). Our focus in this book is not on ideologically inspired questions about the size of the state, what constitutes public sector waste or the relative failings of government versus business. Rather, we are interested in exploring theories and evidence on the efficiency with which vital public services are produced, distributed, planned and allocated. By public services, we mean the systems for the production of public goods for which government is held accountable. These systems can be thought of as policy (or institutional) fields, such as education, health or defence, or specific public organizations, such as schools, hospitals or military units. Decisions that have efficiency implications are made by policy-makers with responsibility for the design of large-scale reforms and by administrators with responsibility for the strategic management of public services. In exploring public service efficiency within these settings, our book is therefore firmly located within the discipline of public administration.

The early history of public administration studies is replete with scholarly concern for the measurement and management of the efficiency of public services (e.g. Walker 1937). However, much of this early interest in efficiency reflected a belief that scientific control of the quantity of production inputs and outputs was needed to eliminate 'waste' in the public sector, and that this goal was the primary value shaping the work of public officials (Mosher 1968). This emphasis on scientific control reflected the notion that the management of public and private organizations was essentially governed by the same universal principles. Drawing upon the ideas of Frederick Taylor, the founding fathers of the discipline of public administration, like Luther Gulick and Lyndall Urwick, devoted their attention to thinking and writing about the ways in which the labour process within government could be made more efficient. Largely absent from this Taylorist discourse was the notion that the democratic underpinning of public administration meant anything more than a responsibility to spend taxpayers' money as sparingly as possible.

For scholars steeped in political science, the connection between politics and the bureaucracy within a properly functioning political system implied a set of democratic principles of administration that were much more substantive than merely controlling the costs of government. According to Dwight Waldo, in particular, efficiency was only one among many administrative values within government, and nowhere near the most important value at that. Instead, democratic ideals, such as service to the public and citizen involvement and participation in government, should take precedence within public administration. Thus, rather than being technical specialists whose function was to improve the ratio of production inputs to outputs, public administrators had a duty to design and implement policies that were somehow responsive to, and even shaped by, public needs and demands.

Waldo's critique of the anti-democratic implications of the science of administrative efficiency continues to dominate contemporary debates about the place of efficiency within public administration (Denhardt and Denhardt 2011; Suleiman 2003); something which the cost-cutting emphasis of NPM has done little to dispel. Beck Jørgenson and Andersen (2011: 336), for example, argue that even in the UK 'the home of NPM ... The dangers of one-sided values and of efficiency crowding out other – classical – values were pointed out'. Despite this on-going hostility towards the value of efficiency, there is an alternative view, which suggests that there are inclusive, far-sighted and democratic elements of the concept of efficient public administration that can guide public managers' decisions about the most appropriate allocation of scarce resources (Grandy 2009; Rutgers and van der Meer 2010).

Rather than downgrading or dodging the efficiency question, our argument in this book is that values such as distributive and intergenerational justice and citizen satisfaction are considerations that should be included within the rubric of a concept of public service efficiency. To reject the pursuit of efficiency as somehow anathema to the aims of government, is to ignore the interplay between democratic values and the hard facts of budgetary constraint and scarce resources that characterize the practice of public administration. In fact, economic theory tells us that market efficiency itself encapsulates more than just the reduction of production costs.

The four faces of efficiency

The annals of economics are replete with discussions about the ways in which properly functioning markets are the most efficient means for supporting a productive economy. According to Samuelson and Nordhaus (2005: 7), markets provide an answer to three 'fundamental' questions societies face when confronting the challenge of economic organization: '*what* commodities are produced, *how* these goods are made, and *for whom* they are produced'. This implies that there is a productive (*how*) dimension to market efficiency, a distributive dimension (*for whom*) and an allocative dimension (*what*). A fourth question – *when* to produce, either now or in the future – can be added to this list, as confirmation that efficiency is not simply static but also has a dynamic longer-term dimension. Economic theory suggests that each of these questions will be answered most efficiently in markets under conditions of perfect competition. Consumers will purchase the goods which most satisfy their preferences, those goods will be produced as cheaply as possible by profit-maximizing firms, whilst resources will be automatically directed to the most socially rewarding uses through the free movement of the factors of production. Freely determined interest rates will take care of the balance between current and future consumption.

Within most economies, the assumptions of perfect competition tend to hold often only with the support of government regulation. Indeed, it is the failure of real-world markets which economists usually regard as providing the rationale for government intervention within the economy. Such intervention may be limited to the establishment of institutions that uphold market competition, but in most countries extends to the provision of services to the general public that the market is unable to supply efficiently. Ironically though, while public service provision may be deemed necessary on the grounds of efficiency, there is no guarantee that government production will itself be any more efficient than the imperfect free market exchanges it replaces (or crowds out) (Moore 1995: 42). Governments everywhere therefore face a public sector efficiency problem, which must be addressed through the conscious application of policy instruments and management reforms designed to improve the functioning of public services.

Following Samuelson, we suggest that there are four main dimensions, or faces (Lukes 1974), of public service efficiency that are the object of public policy and administration within a democracy. The first, *productive efficiency*, relates to the maximization of outputs over inputs; the second, *distributive efficiency*, relates to the equity with which services are distributed between citizens given the budget constraints in the public sector; the third, *dynamic efficiency*, refers to the balance between present and future public service consumption; while the fourth, *allocative efficiency*, refers to the match between the demand for and supply of services. Within this book, we explore the role that each of these different dimensions plays in the theory and practice of public administration. In doing so, we also examine approaches to measuring and managing productive, distributive, dynamic and allocative efficiency.

Measuring and managing efficiency

Since government cannot rely on the free market for the efficient supply of public services, it must seek to manage the provision of those services as efficiently as possible. Within this context, it is conceivable that the skills, expertise and public service ethos of officials might be relied upon as the source of efficiency-enhancing practices. However, there is no *prima facie* reason for supposing that government employees can be trusted to use resources any more efficiently than their private sector counterparts, even if efficiency is espoused by them as a core administrative value. Or, put differently, the incentives for public managers and organizations to provide services as efficiently as possible must be designed into the service production system. Because efficiency must be managed, it becomes correspondingly essential that the results of those managerial efforts be susceptible to evaluation. In the public sector, there are no clear signals from the market that the services being produced are (in)efficient compared to those that are available to private firms, such as profitability, customer satisfaction, market share and, ultimately, bankruptcy. The development and use of appropriate measures of public service efficiency is therefore integral to its management.

The measurement of efficiency in the public sector is an issue that continues to exercise the minds of public economists and public administration scholars. Aside from the question of whether or not what is produced should be measured, debates about efficiency have largely been concerned with determining the best approaches to capturing relevant public service inputs and outputs. In contrast to the private sector that benefits from unambiguous indicators of market efficiency, there are few clear markers of what constitutes efficiency in the public sector. One consequence of this measurement ambiguity is the tendency to regard public service efficiency as simply the optimum ratio between the quantity of inputs and the quantity of outputs. This approach certainly has the merit of being susceptible to measurement and modelling using linear programming techniques, such as Data Envelopment Analysis and Stochastic Frontier Analysis. However, identification of an efficient production frontier often tells one very little about the quality of the public services being produced, whether some consumers should receive more of a service, whether the balance between current and future expenditures is about right or whether or not services are meeting customer demand.

The conceptual difficulties presented by the measurement of each of the four dimensions of efficiency are largely associated with the challenge of developing appropriate indicators of public service outputs. Inputs into the production of public services tend to be more easily conceptualized and measured. Indicators of the cost and volume of labour and capital required to produce public services are readily available and can be easily incorporated within the evaluation of public service efficiency. By contrast, the development of measures of public service outputs is a much more contested activity, principally because of the many perspectives on government activity held by the stakeholders in public service production. Politicians, public managers, professional groups and service users in general, all have different views about what constitute the purpose of public services, and hence have very different notions about what should be considered the main output of any given agency or programme.

Although public service stakeholders may differ in their opinion of what public purposes matter most, they are likely to be in agreement about those elements of public service output that are important to them, if to varying degrees. Broadly speaking, public service outputs have several dimensions that are integral to the four faces of efficiency we have identified: output quantity and output quality (*productive*); equality of opportunity and outcome (*distributive*); the physical, human, intellectual, social and natural capital that public services create (*dynamic*); and customer satisfaction and procedural justice (*allocative*). A variety of indicators can be used by public policymakers and managers to capture these aspects of efficiency, ranging from counts of the sheer number of clients served and efforts to assess output variations across social groups, to proxies for the contribution public services make to national economic growth and surveys gauging the satisfaction of service recipients. Critically, in developing such indicators, it becomes possible not only to analyse levels of public service efficiency, but also to evaluate the impact of policies intended to deliver improvements on each dimension.

Evaluation of the policies and strategies designed to improve efficiency is important for government because it can inform future reforms and initiatives.

It is also an essential means for public officials to meet the democratic demands of their roles by furnishing them with evidence that can be used to publicly justify the adoption of one course of action rather than another. Typically, efficiency-orientated policies are designed to generate improvements to one dimension of efficiency in particular. For productive efficiency, policies generally seek to capture new economies of scale (e.g. mergers), scope (e.g. shared services) or flow (e.g. business process re-engineering). For distributive efficiency, there is usually a concern with tax transfers from the wealthy to the more disadvantaged (e.g. higher rate income tax), targeted social programmes (e.g. urban regeneration schemes) and professional development (e.g. equality and diversity training). Dynamic efficiency is pursued through a myriad of policies ranging from on-going cost–benefit analysis and the establishment of fiscal rules to investments in regional development boards and research and development centres. For allocative efficiency, the focus is usually on citizen voice opportunities (e.g. participation mechanisms), choice (e.g. developing a market of providers) or process (e.g. procedural rules). Of course, these policies are unlikely to result only in changes to a single dimension of efficiency. Instead, there are likely to be a patchwork of efficiency effects across the four dimensions. In fact, management of the emergence of alternative overall efficiency scenarios is one of the core tasks of democratic public administration.

Public service efficiency and democracy

In the past, an emphasis on productive efficiency alone may have blinded public administration scholars to the multiple democratic values, which public managers are expected to realize or at least negotiate in their everyday decision-making (Denhardt 2004; Waldo 1952). An expanded conception of efficiency that captures each of its four faces can illustrate that there is no reason to assume that theorizing about policies for improving efficiency implies the ends of government have become subordinated to administrative means (Denhardt 2004; Du Gay 2008). Even so, there is still a pressing need for the politics of public service efficiency to be incorporated within a framework for its analysis and evaluation. As Hoggett emphasizes (2006: 177), the public realm is a forum for the 'contestation of public purposes', as much as it is the setting for policy action.

Numerous scholars have sought to develop theoretical accounts that bring together an acknowledgement of the need to manage public organizations effectively with the democratic foundations of public administration. Mark Moore's (1995) work on the role that managers can play in creating public value, in particular, draws attention to the myriad democratic values that underpin public service production. For Moore, the creation of public value by public services depends as much upon the use of the intangible resources of the state, especially its legal and moral authority, as the tangible resources, like people and money that typically fall under the efficiency banner. This, in turn, implies that a theory of public service efficiency, however framed, must pay heed to the ways in which public authority is used to create public value.

Liberal political theorists, especially, suggest that the public justification of principles and policies is a requirement of the exercise of political authority within a democracy (Evans 1999). More specifically, John Rawls (1996) argues that advocates of changes to public policy must adhere to an ideal of public reason, whereby any new initiatives should be justified in terms of their contribution to the good of the public as a whole. This, according to Rawls, is not only a regulative principle for ensuring that public policies are not overrun by sectional interests, but is also a 'characteristic of a democratic people: it is the reason of citizens, of those sharing the status of equal citizenship' (1996: 213).

The application of the ideal of public reason to the pursuit of public service efficiency has two important consequences for policy-makers and managers wishing to (re)shape public service production. First, the overarching rationale or objective underpinning policies must be carefully explained. Why is policy change required? How will an intervention lead to improvements in efficiency? Which dimensions of efficiency is the intervention intended to improve? What are the anticipated effects on the other dimensions of efficiency? Second, selection of the advocated approach rather than some other strategy for realizing the anticipated benefits should be justified in accordance with established scientific standards. What do existing studies tell us about the merits of a proposed policy intervention? Are there other initiatives that research suggests may prove more successful? How do the different policy options stack up in terms of the balance of effects across the different dimensions of efficiency? How will the impact of the proposed intervention be evaluated? Taken together, these conditions imply that a commitment to evidence-based policy-making and management is at the heart of democratic public administration.

Structure of the book

In the second chapter we begin our examination of the concept of public service efficiency by exploring the dynamics of the efficiency problem in the public sector. We first consider what economic theory has to say about non-market failure, before reflecting on the potential drivers of efficient government production. We identify four main influences on public service efficiency: the political market, the bureaucracy, the public service motivation of public officials and public management reforms. Rather than elaborating on the philosophical roots of each of these drivers, we focus on what they mean for the efficient production and delivery of public services. In doing so, we also seek to explore how notions of efficiency are reflected in public administration practice.

In chapter three we examine concepts and measures of productive efficiency, focusing in particular on the nature of public service inputs and outputs and offering some thoughts about the ways in which productive efficiency can be measured and managed. We go on to argue that policies to enhance productive efficiency tend to reflect two approaches to managing public services:

first, the economics of production, which stresses the importance of econo-mies of scale, scope and flow; and second, the economics of incentives, which emphasizes the competitive virtues of the free market. A broad overview is offered of the available evidence on the merits of these two contrasting approaches to improving productive efficiency.

In chapter four, we turn our attention to distributive efficiency. Although the notion of productive efficiency addresses the question of whether the ser-vices provided by public organizations are cost-effective, it says nothing about how those services should be distributed among citizens. In democratic poli-tical systems, the distributional equity of public service provision is typically an important consideration. As well as deciding how to produce, government needs to decide who services should be provided for. Or, put differently, whether providing more services to some groups of citizens rather than others may be socially efficient. In such a way, the use of resources to address the needs of relatively deprived groups or areas may be preferred to universal services. We argue that tax-and-spend policies, targeted initiatives, and a range of profes-sional development activities can lead to more distributively efficient public services, and reflect on evidence of the efficacy of these strategies for improving distributive efficiency.

The dimensions of efficiency that are considered in the previous two chapters are all static, in that they consider the management of resources at any given point of time. In chapter five, we examine the concept of dynamic efficiency, which is focused on the distribution of resources between current and future consumption. Capital investment – building schools, hospitals and transport infrastructure – carries the opportunity cost of reduced current consumption, but under-investment now might impede the flow of future benefits. In this chapter, we explore concepts and indicators of dynamic efficiency, before identifying six main areas of capital investment that form the focal point for policies aimed at enhancing this dimension of efficiency: physical, human, intellectual, social and natural capital. We go on to assess the efficiency of government attempts to invest in each of these elements of capital.

Chapter six deals with the issue of allocative efficiency reflecting, in particular, on how government can determine which services citizens would prefer the public sector to provide. We argue that its democratic roots make this dimension of efficiency the most important for policy-makers seeking to improve public service delivery. In economic theory, allocative efficiency refers to the match between the demand for services and their supply. Thus, a service may, in productive terms, be provided very efficiently, but if it is not one that people want, it can still represent an inefficient allocation of resources. In this chap-ter, we suggest that governments tend to rely on three main strategies for improving allocative efficiency: citizen voice opportunities, choice mechanisms and procedural fairness. The evidence on the impact of these strategies is surveyed.

In chapter seven, we explore what it means to manage public services efficiently in a democracy. Given the multiple values inherent in democratic public administration, there is no automatic process which ensures a scenario in which there are improvements across all four dimensions of public service efficiency. In fact, we identify two alternative efficiency scenarios in which there may be highly variable improvements (and deteriorations) to the different dimensions of efficiency. This places a great onus on public policy-makers and managers to develop policies and strategies whose content and likely effects are capable of being justified to citizens. We illustrate how this process of public justification is an essential ingredient in meeting the public sector efficiency problem by drawing on the concept of public reason as a guiding ideal for the conduct of democratic public administration. Case studies from the UK of four policies aimed at improving a single dimension of efficiency each are then used to illustrate the political and managerial challenges associated with different efficiency scenarios.

The final chapter of the book offers a synthesis of all the material presented in the substantive chapters of the book, and explores the theoretical and practical implications of the arguments that we develop. The limitations of what is currently known about public service efficiency are assessed and avenues of efficiency requiring further research identified.

2   The public sector efficiency problem

Although the four dimensions of efficiency we have described are not new other than the productive dimension, they have not received much attention in the public management literature. Indeed, it is our frustration with the way in which public service efficiency has been described and researched which prompted us to write this book. This chapter reviews the established accounts of public service efficiency – both positive and negative – in preparation for our exploration of the four faces in subsequent chapters.

The economic critique of public service efficiency tells us that services owned and operated by government, while justified by reference to the inefficiencies of free markets, are themselves plagued by efficiency problems. The absence of market forces – together with the presence of a series of nonmarket complications – mean that public services will struggle across all four dimensions of efficiency. Productive efficiency will suffer from so called red tape and the lack of pressure to contain costs. Any attempt to address distributive efficiency inevitably causes inequities of its own. Dynamic efficiency is almost impossible to gauge in projects where the return on investment is difficult to valorize. Finally, allocative efficiency is hard to realize when only standard services are offered in the face of diverse preferences.

While acknowledging that public services lack the disciplinary effects of free markets, defenders of the state's role in public service delivery point to a distinctive set of processes which give the state certain efficiency advantages of its own. It is argued, for example, that in a contested political market competing parties will strive to hunt out efficiency savings and increase public value in a bid to improve their offer to the electorate. In such a way, competition between parties for votes may prove an adequate substitute for competition between firms for sales (Wittman 1989). While in terms of the day-to-day business of routine service delivery, it has long been acknowledged that bureaucracies have the capacity to beat the market in terms of their transactions costs (Coase 1937; Williamson 1981). The defenders of the state also point to an increasing body of evidence which suggests that public servants themselves are galvanized by a public service motivation which drives them to work with more devotion than their private sector counterparts (Francois 2000). Finally, alongside these well-established virtues, at least for the last thirty years, governments have down-sized, privatized, marketized, performance managed, reorganized and regulated public services specifically with the intention of improving their economy, efficiency and effectiveness.

This chapter reviews both sides of the efficiency argument. In the first section we consider the economic critique of the public sector which suggests problems across our dimensions of efficiency. Over four sections we then go on to consider the efficiency advantages of public sector delivery which suggest some balance, if not refutation, of the economic critique. We conclude, perhaps not altogether surprisingly, that the theoretical arguments for and against the efficiency of the public sector are evenly balanced. While there are no theoretical grounds to believe that one sector is necessarily superior to another, it is equally clear that neither are their grounds for complacency. Cracks in the institutional arrangements responsible for driving and overseeing public service efficiency mean that politicians and public managers need to be alive to the efficiency challenge – in all of its dimensions – so that they can manage their services accordingly.

The economic critique

While some empirical studies compare the efficiency of the same services across private and public sector service delivery (Vining and Boardman 1992), the critique of public sector efficiency is largely a theoretical one. It is a case which rests, in the first instance, on the absence of market forces. So whereas there are good theoretical reasons to think that free markets will incentivize consumers, employees and entrepreneurs to maximize the value of their individual assets – thereby ensuring efficiency overall – the same incentives are either weak or non-existent in the public realm. But the public sector problem is explained by more than the absence of market forces. As Wolf (1987) explains, the forces of demand and supply for state services still exist, but in the public realm they can all too easily assume a rather peculiar form which has profound implications for efficiency.

In such a way, the *demand* for public services comes, very often, not from the eventual beneficiaries of those interventions but rather from the 'claims making' activity of campaigners – whether they be politicians, public managers, pressure groups or the media – who frame a particular condition as a problem deserving of a government response (Spector and Kitsuse 1977; Entwistle and Enticott 2007). The demand for public interventions is not effective demand as economists define it – in terms of a willingness and capacity to pay – rather, it is a notional demand premised on the presumption that someone else (government) or everyone else (through taxation) will pick up the bill. This decoupling of potential beneficiaries from willingness to pay means that the demand for public services may, as the economic jargon puts it, suffer from free-rider problems. With no individual budget constraint, the demand for public services of one form or another is without limit, this makes it a very different thing to the demand normally described by economists, as Downs explains (1966: 30): 'There is no mechanism for matching the taxes paid by each citizen with the utility he receives from government activity'.

Supply is also problematic. While campaigners may agree on the case for intervention in broad terms, the specification of intended outputs and outcomes often remains unclear. On the supply side then the 'technology', as Wolf (1987: 61) describes it, 'of producing non-market outputs is frequently unknown, or if known, is associated with considerable uncertainty and ambiguity'. Without the clarity of a concrete product, and sometimes even an identifiable consumer, public service providers control performance through detailed specification of the processes of delivery. While, as we will see later, the bureaucratic form promises a number of advantages, it has the fundamental disadvantage that service delivery is only as good as the rules that guide it. But the application of these rules can, as Merton (1940: 563) puts it, easily collapse into ritualism where there is 'an unchallenged insistence upon punctilious adherence to formalised procedure'. Bozeman (1993) identifies thirteen ways in which the writing or implementation of these rules can go wrong. When they do, public service providers end up with unnecessary or dysfunctional rules – red tape – rather than efficient processes. A situation often compounded by the fact that governments very often entrust the supply of state services to a single agency in a way that gives them a monopoly in their jurisdiction and of course a budget which is negotiated, for the reasons we have described, largely without reference to robust measures of performance. The dysfunctional nature of public service demand and supply gives rise to problems across all four faces of efficiency.

First, Wolf (1987: 64) argues that government activities – whether in the form of 'regulation, administering transfer payments or direct production of public goods' – will be more prone to 'technically inefficient production' than their market equivalents. Services will be provided more expensively than necessary for a number of reasons. As we have seen, state-owned enterprises often enjoy a monopoly and therefore lack any pressure on prices from competitors. Furthermore, because 'the revenues that sustain an activity are unrelated to the cost of producing it' (Wolf 1987: 64), it is all too easy for more resources than necessary to be used in production. With little agreement on anticipated outcomes – but with the discretionary space and resources to gold-plate production processes – public managers may, as Santerre (1986: 55) explains, 'use public resources to maximise their personal utility'. Niskanen (1973: 22) anticipates bureaucrats perpetually seeking to maximize their budgets and the 'salary, perquisites of the office, public reputation, power, patronage' that go with it. Finally, with poorly defined conditions of demand and supply, Wolf (1987: 64) concludes that 'if technological possibilities exist for lowering cost functions, raising productivity, or realizing economies of scale, these opportunities are more likely to be ignored or less likely to be exploited fully by nonmarket than market activities'.

Second, Wolf's (1987) analysis alerts us to the likely problems of distributive efficiency. While many government interventions are justified in terms of correcting the inequity of free market distributions of income, wealth and opportunity, governments can still make matters worse. First, in the very business of making society governable, the state intentionally creates 'huge differences in power and privilege' (Wolf 1987: 66) which advantage some but disadvantage others. While the grant of authority may be extended on terms most of us accept, it is unlikely to be regarded as just by everybody at all times. Second, policies may have unintended distributional consequences in terms of over-rewarding particular groups or else crowding out free market transactions which would otherwise occur. The European Union's attempts to regulate agricultural production, for example, clearly translate into substantial subsidies for some and correlative costs for others. Whether the redistribution of resources wrought by this intervention is more just than that which would prevail in its absence is, of course, a debatable point.

Third, problems of dynamic efficiency emerge from the different timescales and interests of elected politicians and society. With relatively short periods of office, politicians will be inclined to overvalue benefits today and undervalue future benefits and costs. The result, as Wolf (1987: 55–56) puts it, is 'an appreciable disjuncture between the short time horizons of political actors, and the longer time required to analyze, experiment and understand a particular problem'. Rather than making wise long-term investment decisions, the reverse might be the case. Elected politicians have few incentives to make budget decisions today which will bear fruit long after they have left office or, indeed, to confront problems which will incur more costs than benefits in the short term. In such a way the electoral cycle of democratic politics might incline politicians to favour short-term vanity projects – like Tony Blair's infamous Millennium Dome – over the resolution of long-term problems like global warming. Dynamic efficiency is further plagued by the difficulty of attaching values to the benefits which flow from investment decisions. Almost by definition, the state is called to make investment decisions – which will incur substantial short-term costs but promise only delayed, uncertain and diffuse benefits – for which it is institutionally ill-equipped.

Finally, problems of allocative efficiency emerge from the nature of public goods (Hart and Cowhey 1977: 351). They are, as the economic jargon puts it, 'lumpy' in that many public services 'must be provided in a fixed amount or quantity to produce positive benefits' (Thompson 1987: 433–34). 'Half a lighthouse', as Thompson goes on to explain, 'is, perhaps, worse than useless, more than one is redundant'. Lumpy public services, set against the infinite variety of public preferences mean almost inevitably, that many citizens will be left dissatisfied by the service they receive (Weisbrod 1997). Even if the political system is working as its advocates suggest, the tax-service package will strike the right balance only for the median voter. Problems are further exacerbated by the gap between the 'elusive' social goals informing the case for government intervention on the one hand and the 'private organizational goals' which are used by managers to 'guide, regulate and evaluate' agency and employee performance on the other (Wolf 1987: 65). In simple terms this means that while there may be broad agreement and support for the official or public purposes of a government organization, it is all too easy for governments to produce the wrong services, in the wrong quantity and at the wrong price (in terms of the taxes or charges that it levies on citizens).

This rather depressing account of the prospects for public sector efficiency needs to be weighed against the case developed by the defenders of the state. It is not exactly surprising that when measured against the benchmarks of freely interacting demand and supply – and assuming that public servants are as entrepreneurial in their pursuit of self-advantage as are free market entrepreneurs – state services will be found wanting. The whole point of state intervention is that it is prompted by different forms of motivation and in turn regulated by a very distinctive set of processes, to those which prevail in free markets. These differences in motivation and process, at least on the face of it, suggest that the state might have some advantages in the efficiency game. A balanced assessment of public service efficiency needs to consider these nonmarket drivers of efficiency. We look at these under four headings.

The political market

Although public services are not ruled by the free markets, they are subject to a different set of controls intended to ensure their efficiency. In democratic governments this system is based on representative democracy and open accountability. Some commentators suggest that when political forces are given free rein and political institutions are appropriately designed, a liberal democracy can provide an adequate substitute for the disciplining effects of market forces. Wittman (1989: 1395–96) argues that: 'democratic political markets are organized to promote wealth-maximizing outcomes, that these markets are highly competitive, and that political entrepreneurs are rewarded for efficient behavior.'

The theory is straightforward (see Dunleavy 1991 for a review). While public services are not bought and sold in the same way as private services, votes are traded in an analogous way. In an effort to win votes and secure election, politicians prepare tax-service packages which they believe will be attractive to electors. By winning the votes of citizens, the politicians with the most attractive package will win the election and implement their manifesto, thus ensuring that the public services provided by governments match the preferences of citizens. Elections also give electors the opportunity to reflect on the performance of incumbents, so that politicians who are perceived as failing to match the tax and service preferences of citizens – failing, in other words, to ensure efficiency – will be punished at the polls. In such a way, political competition between elites will ensure that any waste and inefficiency is quickly identified and removed.

To work at its best, competition between would-be representatives needs to take place against the backdrop of transparent reporting of public spending and performance. Where public organizations are open about their performance and the ways in which they spend public money, both politicians and citizens are better placed to make judgements about the management of public services. There is a long-established tradition of openly reporting some of the most important economic indicators of national performance including budgets, growth, unemployment and so forth. New developments in technology allow scrutiny to be extended across a broader range of issues and to a much greater depth allowing, sometimes, the forensic investigation of the decisions taken by individual public servants. Alongside political competitors, the media, campaign groups and engaged citizens, a host of state regulatory and audit bodies have been established with the explicit purpose of hunting out and reporting on waste and inefficiency. In the UK there are very few areas of public expenditure which are not subject to the oversight and scrutiny of at least one dedicated agency. These bodies – including, for example, the National Audit Office, the Office for Standards in Education and the Care Quality Commission – crawl over published information and primary data of their own in a search for glaring examples of waste and inefficiency. The evidence collected in this way is then publicized, and sometimes re-scrutinized in more theatrical terms, by political opponents in a bid to out-manoeuvre incumbents.

Although superficially plausible, the political market model has weaknesses. Unlike free markets, which are made up of innumerable individual transactions, opportunities for political transactions are few and far between. Liberal democracies typically provide large and diverse populations with single governments, elected only infrequently often on rather disappointing turnouts. Lumpy goods designed for the median voter – even when subject to the intensive scrutiny processes we have described – are likely to leave large tracts of the population dissatisfied by the tax-service package. This problem can be mitigated to some degree by democratic reforms. Devolution to smaller units of government at the regional, local, even neighbourhood level, and increases in the frequency of opportunities for the expression of voice – through more frequent elections, referendums, consultation initiatives and so forth – should all have the effect of increasing the responsiveness of the political system to the preferences of citizens. Indeed, as we shall see in chapter six, there is some evidence that where more opportunities for voice are provided, the greater is the restraint applied by voters. Voters do care about efficiency and will use the ballot box to communicate that interest. Some argue that developments in information and communication technologies mean that democratization can be taken much further. Margolis (1979), for example, argues that traditional approaches to direct and representative democracy are fundamentally ill-suited to the challenge of governing the complex mass societies of the contemporary world, and that a range of new technologies of participation may be required. Updating the argument, Dunleavy *et al.* (2006) claim that information and communication technologies have already prompted the birth of 'digital era governance' in which citizens can participate in the business of government on an unprecedented scale and depth.

The political market model further assumes that parties will compete to understand and then deliver the preferences of electors. The reality, of course, is that the democratic market place is as subject to imperfections and distortions as the private market for goods and services. The vagaries of the electoral system, combined with domination by a few political parties, may mean that electors are presented with only a limited range of alternatives. Indeed, the contest for the median voter may mean that parties offer near indistinguishable proposals for taxes and services and long periods of consensus in which changes in the governing party make little difference to the policies pursued (Kavanagh 1985), a situation likely to be compounded by resource differences resulting from the advantage of incumbency, which make it very difficult for smaller parties, or interests, to challenge the status quo. Incumbents, by contrast – enjoying the benefit of considerable state power – may be able to turn the democratic process on its head and shape the preferences of electors to accord with their own priorities (Dunleavy 1991).

It is undoubtedly true that the accountability mechanisms and democratic competition we have described ensure that public services get more scrutiny than do their private counterparts. It is inconceivable that the line-by-line justification of expense claims – increasingly required of public managers and politicians in the UK – would ever be seen in the private sector. But then the drivers of efficiency are very different. Although public services and levels of taxation are subject to considerable scrutiny and political debate, it is not clear that these processes are, by themselves, a sufficient substitute for the contestability of free markets. There are a number of ways in which the will of the electorate can be lost in translation or else reshaped at birth. But democracy is not the only driver of efficiency in the public sector.

The promise of bureaucracy

Even if we assume that our representatives genuinely reflect our preferences, the efficiency of state-owned services further presumes that politicians are served by a neutral administrative machine which will translate political commitments into public services as cost effectively as possible. It is to that question that we now turn. Although governments intervene in the economy and society in a number of different ways – procuring services through free markets and persuading citizens to change behaviour voluntarily (Bell *et al.* 2010) – all their interventions have, at least since the mid-19th century, been underwritten by the logic of bureaucratic organization. Simply put, government intervention is premised on the idea of a legitimate central authority which plans and scripts the actions of subordinate agents to deliver intended outcomes.

In the UK, the central planks of the bureaucratic model were established by the Northcote and Trevelyan report of 1854. Northcote and Trevelyan's prescription for a permanent bureaucracy was informed by a 'series of investigations over the previous five years into the organisation of various departments to ensure both efficiencies and economies' (Greenaway 2004: 2). The traditional system in which politicians appointed friends and family to do their bidding was widely seen as inefficient and unreliable. Barratt quotes Sir Robert Peel as complaining 'of the excessive time that was required to devote to dealing with correspondence from relatives anxious to secure positions for their kinsfolk in the offices of government' (Barratt 2009: 69). The 'intellectual elite' envisaged by Northcote and Trevelyan 'fitted the bill for the new political order after 1870' in which civil servants 'could develop a role as "neutral" dispassionate advisers to their political masters' (Greenaway 2004: 11–12).

A number of aspects of bureaucratic organization suit the interventions of democratic governments. First, bureaucracy promises rationality. As citizens and employees, we buy into hierarchical structures because we believe that they are guided by rational decisions. Markets provide space for individual rationality but no way of handling the collective action problems which provide the justification for state intervention. Second, bureaucracy promises, although it does not always deliver, clear lines of control and responsibility allowing politicians – and in turn their electors – to maintain control. Finally, where rationality or control fail, bureaucracy provides the audit trail necessary for accountability so that electors can, as Carroll Quigley famously put it, 'throw the rascals out' (1966: 1248). Taken together – rationality, control and accountability – make bureaucracy a uniquely reassuring form of organization. Reassuring maybe, but is bureaucracy efficient?

Certainly Weber thought so, or more precisely the Parsons translation of Weber suggests that he did. According to Parsons, Weber concluded that: 'Experience tends universally to show that the purely bureaucratic type of administrative organization—that is, the monocratic variety of bureaucracy— is, from a purely technical point of view, capable of attaining the highest degree of efficiency' (Weber 1947: 337). Gajduschek (2003) argues, however, that Weber did not actually use the word efficiency, and even if he had, he could not have had in mind the specific definitions of efficiency developed since. It is clear though that Weber did not regard bureaucracy as prone to the inefficiencies rehearsed by public choice theorists. Rather as Pugh, Hickson and Hinings (1971: 22) explain, he seemed to be drawn towards the notion of a machine in which: 'Precision, speed, unambiguity, knowledge of files, continuity, discretion, unity, strict subordination, reduction of friction and of material and personal costs – these are raised to the optimum point'.

In marked contrast to free markets – in which the dogged pursuit of self-interest drives the emergence of economic efficiency – bureaucracies owe their efficiency to the dispassionate service of public servants. Without the impassive machine which implements the rules and processes of government 'without affection or enthusiasm', as Du Gay (2008: 339) puts it, 'the whole apparatus of the state would disintegrate'. But it is not only the state that relies on bureaucracy for technical efficiency. Indeed it is this form of coordination which all large private sector organizations – from Ford to McDonalds – adopt when they need to organize the delivery of standard products and services. The domination of large organizations is in many ways attributable to the efficiency advantages of the bureaucratic form of organization. Under the title the *McDonaldization of Society*, Ritzer (1983: 100) describes bureaucratic processes emphasizing 'efficiency, predictability, calculability, substitution of nonhuman for human technology, and control over uncertainty' as penetrating almost every aspect of life.

Alongside Weber, Coase (1937) too, argues that the hierarchical form of organization promises a series of advantages over the market alternative. More specifically, he explains that organizing through markets incurs a 'cost of discovering what the relevant prices' are, a 'cost of negotiating and concluding a separate contract' and a cost of uncertainty implicit in any long-term commitment (Coase 1937: 390–92). Williamson (1981) has extended this analysis by identifying a whole series of conditions – including the specificity of assets and the frequency of use – which determine the costs of a transaction. Taken together these considerations, again at least in theory, can give the centralized decision-making processes of bureaucracy a considerable cost advantage compared to organization through free markets.

Again, we know of course, that this account is open to theoretical critique: rational decision-making, at least in formal terms, is impossible; rules, as we have seen, can easily collapse into red tape; communication and accountability can be distorted by bewildering complexity (Merton 1940; Simon 1944). Bureaucratic officials may be not capable, or inclined, to the studied neutrality described by Du Gay (2008), perhaps using the opportunities provided by imperfect oversight to advance their own interests above those of their political masters (Dunleavy 1991). Empirically too, the bureaucratic model has repeatedly been found not to measure up to the high standards suggested by Weber (Weber 1947; Selznick 1966; Pressman and Wildavsky 1973). The defenders of public service efficiency do not however rest their case solely on democracy and bureaucracy.

Public service motivation

Whereas bureaucracy promises to deliver efficiency through the neutrality of its officials, public service motivation theories suggest that whether by virtue of the nurture provided by their professional socialization or by the intrinsic nature of their values (Pandey and Stazyk 2008), those working in the public services as professionals, officials or managers are 'public spirited altruists' (Le Grand 1997: 149) or 'principled agents' (DiIulio 1994). Knights rather than knaves (Le Grand 1997), public servants can be relied upon to be focused on the public rather than individual interest and to work harder and more imaginatively than their private sector equivalents. From this perspective, public service efficiency is guaranteed not by political scrutiny, or by the rationality of bureaucracy, but by the good will of the men and women who work for the state.

The altruistic account of public servants has its roots in the work of Durkheim and Weber (Parsons 1939) who portrayed the professions more broadly as occupational communities galvanized by a sense of vocation or commitment to the service of their clients or society (Evetts 2003). The expansion of the state in the nineteenth and twentieth centuries provided fertile ground for the birth and development of numerous public service professions in the civil service, planning, social work, teaching and so forth (Perkin 1989). The vocation, or public service motivation, of new recruits was fostered and sustained through a series of tactics long taken to be the defining characteristics or traits of an established profession (Ritzer 1975). A variety of institutional arrangements embracing long periods of education, ethical codes and elaborate mechanisms for oversight and discipline, reassured society that the profession, and the individuals who practised under its banner, were both expert and trustworthy (Carr-Saunders and Wilson 1933; Caplow 1954). The 'success of the claim to professional status is governed', according to Wilensky (1964: 140) 'by the degree to which the practitioners conform to a set of moral norms' defined as 'devotion to the client's interests more than personal or commercial profit'.

While an 'altruistic motivation to serve the interests of a community of people, a state, a nation or humankind' (Rainey and Steinbauer 1999: 20) is not unique to public employees, public service motivation theorists maintain that altruistic motivation is stronger in public than private employment. In such a way, the public service motivation of state officials may give state services an efficiency advantage over the free market. This could happen in two ways. First, a strong public service motivation may mean that public officials are focused on the good stewardship of scarce public resources. They may then be more attentive or imaginative in their search for public value. Alternatively, a strong public service motivation may mean that public officials shirk less, work longer hours or else require lower levels of remuneration than their private equivalents. Francois explains: 'Public sector employees, who are motivated by public service motivation, are thus seen as volunteering a portion of their services to the community for free' (Francois 2000: 276).

Work conducted in this area suggests some support for the public service motivation hypothesis. Crewson (1997: 512) finds that 'public employees with a preference for service over economic benefits are likely to be more committed to agency operations than employees with a preference for economic rewards'. Brewer (2003: 20) finds that 'in addition to their formal job roles ... public servants often perform a variety of extra role behaviours described in terms of citizen engagement. These activities are crucial in forming and sustaining social capital in society at large'. Dilulio's (1994: 282) case study of the US Bureau of Prisons suggests, as he puts it, that 'principled agents are the rule, not the exception, and have been for most of the agency's sixty-three-year history'.

But while there is evidence that public service motivation is stronger in public than private employment (Boyne 2002a), and of an association with individual performance (Wright 2007), there is little empirical work which finds a relationship between public service motivation and organizational performance (Perry *et al.* 2010), much less of an association with organizational efficiency. Indeed, there are some reasons to think that the reverse might be the case. In a nice development of Niskanen's notion of the budget maximizing bureaucrat, Moynihan (2013) suggests that bureaucrats might seek to maximize their budget because 'they sincerely believe in the benefit of their programs.' Strong public service motivation combined with an imperfect budget constraint, may lead public employees to improve services beyond the level appreciated by citizens, or perhaps to over-provide those services which they would prefer citizens to receive. Thus, a theory of altruistic public service motivation is not the same as a theory of public service efficiency; indeed as Moynihan suggests, it might be the reverse.

Public choice theorists argue that far from government being immune from naked self-interest, there are good reasons to think that both politicians and officials will behave in exactly the same way as free market individualists. Drawing on Samuelson's assumption of maximizing agents, Niskanen (1973) imagines bureaucrats seeking to perpetually maximize their bureaucracy, while Downs (1957) assumes that politicians will seek only to maximize their votes. Without the checks provided by free market competition, public choice theorists describe individual self-interest as capable of producing profoundly dysfunctional effects. Dilulio (1994: 278) colourfully characterizes the public choice position as assuming that 'most bureaucrats behave not as public-spirited souls but as self-seeking slugs who are disposed to shirk, subvert, and steal whenever and wherever they can get away with it.'

The new public management

In truth, the day-to-day world of the contemporary public manager might seem somewhat removed from the traditional theories of democracy, bureaucracy and public service motivation. Since at least the 1980s, governments across the world have adopted a series of reforms – very often inspired by techniques coined in private management – to improve the efficiency of public services (Hood 1991). While the traditional mechanisms are still important, they need to be seen in the context of this reform agenda. Indeed, to consider the efficiency of the contemporary public sector is as much to inquire into the effectiveness of the New Public Management (NPM) as it is to question the workings of the traditional institutions of representative politics, bureaucracy and public service motivation.

While commentators differ in the ingredients they attribute to the NPM, the privatization of functions no longer viewed as requiring state ownership is prominent in most lists. A host of services – including energy, water, communications and transport – have been moved altogether from the public to the private sector in a number of countries. Others – including hospital and school cleaning, catering and a range of back office functions – while continuing to be funded by taxation, have been contracted out to a rapidly expanding industry of private companies specializing in the delivery of public services. Where full-scale privatization, or some form of contracting, are perceived as inappropriate – the rump of state-owned service providers including education and health – have been marketized to different degrees by establishing them as free-standing business units or agencies of one form or another which have to sell their wares to client organizations or users empowered to choose their provider of choice.

At the same time, the old insistence on due process associated with bureaucratic forms of control has increasingly been displaced by forms of 'remote control' based on performance indicators and external regulation (Hoggett 1991: 245). Public organizations find themselves inspected and graded against centrally determined performance criteria and then named and shamed or praised accordingly. Models of funding have also changed, as block grants are replaced by a new enthusiasm for payment by results in which public service providers – of public, private and voluntary sector origin – are rewarded on condition of their delivery of pre-determined outputs and outcomes (Boyne and Chen 2006).

Informed partly by the public choice critique described at the start of this chapter, but also by the challenges presented by a more difficult fiscal environment, governments have adopted these reforms precisely because they believed that public services could be delivered more efficiently. In so far as it is possible to discern a guiding thread running through the NPM – and in truth there may be two or three rather than one – it is the attempt to introduce the very market incentives diagnosed as missing from traditionally organized state-sponsored supply. The key weaknesses giving rise to nonmarket failures – the absence of contestability, weak or ambiguous measures of performance and formula increases in funding – have been challenged if not always changed by the new public management.

The advocates of these reforms maintain that they have transformed the public sector and unleashed a new wave of public entrepreneurialism. Hodge (1998: 98) concludes that 'the weight of evidence appears to support the notion that, on average, the unit cost of services is reduced through competitive tendering of public services'. Osborne and Gaebler (1992), describe a series of case studies in which public servants find new ways of solving problems often at a fraction of the cost of traditional forms of bureaucratic delivery. Moore (1994: 297) picks up the baton in his account of a search for public value which sees managers achieve their 'purposes as efficiently and effectively as possible'. Although the quantitative studies are more equivocal, certainly some of them point to significant cost savings resulting from the contracting out of public services (Andrews 2010).

While this is not the place for an evaluation of the effectiveness of this reform agenda (Andrews 2010), suffice to say that it would be unwise to assume that the NPM has transformed the public sector in quite the manner described by some of its strongest advocates. This is unlikely for a number of reasons. First, the NPM reform agenda is ambivalent and conflicted (Aucoin 1990). While some policies encourage service providers to focus on and respond to the market, other elements reinforce traditional forms of hierarchical control. In such a way, accountability has often been confused rather than clarified. With multiple accountabilities – to customers, partners, regulators, and local, regional and national politicians – it is not always clear which stakeholders managers should be working to satisfy. Second, the conversion to the NPM has been incomplete. Rather than replacing the forms of public management established in the nineteenth century, the new reforms have been layered upon existing forms of management in sometimes 'deeply uncomfortable ways' (Newman and Clarke 2009: 6). Contemporary public management is not then properly old or new, it is a hybrid of the two. Third, the evolution of approaches to governance has not stopped with the NPM. In part reacting to the deficiencies of the NPM but also in response to new challenges – commentators have started to describe new epochs variously dubbed the 'new public governance' or 'public value management' – which emphasize collaboration across agencies and co-production with citizens (Denhardt and Denhardt 2011; Osborne 2006; Stoker 2006; Ashworth and Entwistle 2010).

Conclusion

Four conclusions emerge from this chapter. First, with very different drivers of efficiency in the public and private sectors, it is clear that in theoretical terms we cannot assume that either necessarily has an efficiency advantage over the other. They are apples and pears; while insulated from the drivers of efficiency we see in free markets, state-sponsored services are pushed and pulled by forces of their own, forces which have become increasingly intense and complicated in recent years. While we know that both democracy and bureaucracy sometimes disappoint, their dysfunctions do not necessarily make them less efficient than organization through free markets.

Second, by the same token, it is clear that we cannot dismiss the public sector problem and assume that everything in the efficiency garden is rosy. We already know that it would be unwise to assume that either the traditional model of democracy and bureaucracy or the quasi-market reforms which have been layered onto them, will automatically and inevitably prompt public organizations to operate efficiently. A number of cracks in the model can explain a disjuncture between the tax-service package which citizens want and the tax-service package that they get. Indeed, while there is merit in all four of the drivers of public service efficiency we have considered in this chapter, they do not necessarily work well together. There are tensions between democracy and bureaucracy, bureaucracy and public service motivation, and between public service motivation and the market-like reforms associated with the NPM. Even in purely theoretical terms, it is difficult to see how these mechanisms – and others besides – can coincide in entirely positive terms.

Third, while it is true that the public service efficiency problem has assumed much greater salience in the recent past, the policies adopted to address the problem have been skewed towards the productive dimension of efficiency. The domination of productive efficiency over the other dimensions can be attributed to a number of causes. Productive efficiency is perhaps the easiest of the four dimensions to grasp. It fits most comfortably with the way in which we have traditionally understood and organized our public services and allows relatively straightforward comparisons with the private sector. It promises quick and clearly quantifiable results while leaving the service improvement question safely in the hands of professional managers and politicians. But while the NPM's exhortation to manage government more like a business (Boyne 2002a) may have improved productive efficiency by changing *how* public services are delivered, it has ignored other equally important dimensions.

Finally, beyond the question of *how* to deliver services, lie important questions about *what, for whom* and *when* public services should be provided, which are at least as important, and in some cases rather more so. By focusing singularly on the productive dimension of efficiency, NPM reforms are repeatedly accused of spawning unintended consequences in other dimensions of public service performance. Efforts to cut costs and save money can all too easily lead to a decline in the quality of services or calls for additional administration in other parts of the same organization (O'Toole and Meier 2004a), problems which may, ironically, result in public organizations once more having to correct for market failure by contracting services back in (Hefetz and Warner 2004). In overlooking other, equally important dimensions of efficiency, NPM has had a further effect of turning large numbers of commentators and stakeholders away from the efficiency agenda altogether. Critics assert that an emphasis on productive rationality blinds the advocates of efficiency to the multiple democratic values, which public managers are expected to realize or at least negotiate in their everyday decision-making (Denhardt 2004; Waldo 1952). According to these scholars, an obsession with reducing the costs associated with the delivery of public services implies the dangerous elevation of administrative means above the ends of government (Denhardt 2004; Kingsley 1945; Du Gay 2008). To see the public realm purely in terms of the 'delivery of goods and services', as Hoggett (2006: 177) puts it, is to obscure its role as a forum for the 'contestation of public purposes' and the containment of 'social anxieties'.

While we have some considerable sympathy for this position, we do not think that the concept of productive efficiency should be thrown out with the new public management bath water. Indeed, before we can develop the case for other faces or dimensions of efficiency, we need to be clear about how far the notion of productive efficiency can take us. It is to this task that we now turn.

3 Productive efficiency

The ability of government to carry out its responsibilities as effectively as possible within the constraints of a pre-determined budget is one of the most enduring issues within the theory and practice of public policy and administration (Grandy 2009). The idea that public money can and should always be spent wisely means that the attention paid to the issue of efficiency by those outside government can be somewhat one-eyed, with a heightened sensitivity to the apparent wastefulness of feckless bureaucrats, and the labyrinthine rules and regulations that stymie innovation and good customer service. As a result, public debates about the efficiency of public services are almost without exception debates about the apparent inability of the public sector to provide services as cost-effectively as private sector organizations (Downs and Larkey 1986). Indeed, it is this basic hypothesis that has lain behind most of the public management reforms of the past thirty years (Pollitt and Bouckaert 2011). Yet, behind the noisy rhetoric about government waste and inefficiency lies the deadly serious question of how to deliver affordable improvements in the vital public services upon which so many citizens rely.

Crudely speaking, one might say that the concept of productive efficiency refers to the relative inputs required to achieve the basic outputs of production. So, for example, the number of hours that a teacher spends in a classroom with a designated number of high school students prior to their sitting their graduation examination is an indicator of productive efficiency. Here gains in productive efficiency could clearly be achieved by reducing either the contact time or by increasing the class size. However, in both cases, the quality of the education that students receive may in fact deteriorate, and, in turn, the system output (educated students) may also be jeopardized. This crude example highlights that the measurement of productive efficiency in the public sector is as important as its management. Indeed, defining and measuring inputs and outputs is something that is particularly challenging in the public sector where many of the services are extremely labour-intensive and there is no natural upper bound on the desirable quantity or quality of the service provided.

In democratic societies, the goals of public service organizations are determined by key stakeholders through a complex interaction of economic, political and social considerations. Economically speaking, it is difficult to publicly justify government expenditures, which involve paying a higher price for any given product than would be charged in the open market. And, of course, citizens tend to put some kind of (imagined) premium on the amount that they are willing (or able) to pay government to uphold the public goods they are unable to club together to produce. However, many social needs can only be addressed by government action, which may require costly interventions that are not always the source of popular political support. This places a great onus on public managers and organizations to demonstrate that services are being provided at an acceptable cost. It also implies that policy-makers and public managers should devote time and thought to the ways in which the ratio between outputs and inputs can be continuously improved.

In the case of productive efficiency, what is at stake is the adoption of those policies and practices that are most likely to enable public services to get core tasks done as effectively as possible within the bounds of an acceptable minimum of financial outlay. Policy-makers and administrators (and politicians and voters) choose between alternative desirable public service goals, some of which they may value so greatly that they are willing to pay a cost-inefficient price; though this inevitably means the 'overspend' must be recouped somewhere else within the service production system. Throughout the course of those deliberations, budgetary constraints mean that considerations of productive efficiency play a persistent and necessary part in the decision-making process.

To explore the nature of the pursuit of productive efficiency in public services, we examine what productive efficiency means when applied to the production of goods and services by public organizations. In doing so, we consider how productive efficiency can be measured and the ways in which government generally seeks to maximize outputs and minimize inputs within the public sector. This chapter therefore begins with a discussion of the concept of productive efficiency, focusing particularly on its place within the discipline of public administration. Following that, alternative approaches to measuring and modelling productive efficiency are weighed up, and a schema for its evaluation is developed. Thereafter, evidence on the impact of different approaches to improving productive efficiency is reviewed and conclusions are drawn about the effectiveness of those varying approaches.

What is productive efficiency?

The notion that the maximization of outputs over inputs is an important administrative value in government has a long pedigree (Rutgers and van der Meer 2010). The origins of contemporary concepts of public service efficiency can be traced to the influential Progressive Era of social, political and economic reform in the United States. During this period, numerous liberal reformers succumbed to the belief that rational planning was necessary to eliminate waste within the economy, society and government, as well as to positively enhance the quality of life of citizens (Williams 2003). Scientific study of the causes and consequences of inefficient administration within each of these sectors would therefore enable experts to identify and design technical solutions to social problems (Mosher 1968).

Despite the close interest paid by social and political reformers to the measurement of municipal outputs and outcomes, the first systematic exposition of the concept of efficiency emerged from Frederick Taylor's studies of the manufacturing process. According to Taylor (1911) it was possible to derive universal principles of efficient work design by amassing a wealth of information about the work routines of individual employees, especially in terms of the amount of time that was required for them to produce a given unit of output. By comparing the performance of individual workers, it would then become apparent what standards it was reasonable to expect workers to attain, and hence what constituted efficient production and the level of training and supervision required to achieve this. Although Taylor's work was largely carried out in manufacturing plants, he nonetheless believed it applicable to any organizational setting, including government. Indeed, he vigorously argued that the scientific organization of government could only be achieved by elevating the principle of efficiency above normative political values (Taylor 1916).

Taylor's ideas came to influence the work of key public administration scholars such as Luther Gulick and Lyndall Urwick (1937) who believed there to be universal rules governing the maximization of outputs over inputs. According to Urwick (1937: 49), 'there are certain principles which govern the association of human beings for any purpose, just as there are certain engineering principles which govern the building of a bridge'. In the case of public administration, productive efficiency was therefore the 'fundamental value upon which the science of administration may be erected' (Gulick 1937: 193). By this, Gulick meant, as Taylor did before him, that considerations of efficiency were more important than those of democracy – at least for public managers (Denhardt 2004).

This theme of the maximization of outputs over inputs was later taken up by Herbert Simon (1976: 179) who argued that 'efficiency dictates that choice of alternatives which produce the largest result for the given application of resources'. This stress on results highlights that the concept of productive efficiency not only incorporates notions of economy – the reduction of costs – but also those of effectiveness – the maximization of outputs. Hence, productive efficiency implies the effort to simultaneously pursue the maximization of outputs and the minimization of inputs (Farrell 1957). Simon (1976: 188), in particular, stresses that 'the problem of efficiency is to find the maximum of a production function; with the constraint that total expenditure is fixed'. To determine the shape of a public service production function, it is important to be able to draw upon valid and reliable measures of inputs and outputs.

Measuring productive efficiency

The measurement of productive efficiency in the public sector is an issue that continues to be debated at great length by economists and statisticians (e.g. Atkinson 2005; Boyle 2006; Diewert 2011). In fact, defining and measuring the inputs and outputs of public service production has long been recognized to be critically important yet fraught with conceptual and political complexities that are not easily resolved by policy-makers and analysts (Simpson 2009). That said, such an endeavour is central to any attempt to analyse how, and in what ways, public services might be made more productively efficient.

Inputs

To develop a comprehensive overview of the productive efficiency of any given public service, it is essential to measure the full range of inputs and processes involved in the provision of that service. Public organizations deliver a bewildering array of different services, from the giant machine bureaucracies that process tax returns and vehicle licenses, right through to the rapid response teams that deal with serious accidents and emergencies, and the highly personalized individual care provided in nursing homes. To maximize output in each of these services within their budget constraint, public managers will be required to bring into play a whole range of different types of input and make informed decisions about the quantity of each input required to attain desired levels of output. Critically, those inputs can be either *endogenous* (i.e. internal to a public organization), such as the cost of employing qualified teachers to educate children and the number of hours of teaching required to produce a given educational output, or *exogenous* (i.e. external to the organization), such as the number of hours parents spend reading books with children at home.

Endogenous resource inputs

The endogenous inputs into the provision of public services typically consist of the costs and volume of the human and physical capital utilized in service production. Indeed, one common way in which the work of public services is distinguished is the extent to which it can be characterized as either labour or capital intensive. The provision of education, health, social care, housing and a whole gamut of other distributive public services require the contribution of qualified professional staff and the corresponding paraphernalia of human resources support. By contrast, the provision of transportation infrastructure, environmental protection, emergency response and other regulatory services requires much greater usage and maintenance of technology, buildings and equipment. To evaluate the productive efficiency of any given public service it is therefore essential to draw upon indicators that are able to capture the degree of labour and capital intensity in service production.

Input indicators associated with the pursuit of productive efficiency in labour-intensive public service provision include: salary costs for professional, administrative, technical and ancillary staff; temporary staffing costs; human resource management systems; travel and subsistence expenses and so on. Input indicators associated with the on-going costs of capital-intensive public service provision include: software costs; research and development needs; procurement systems; performance management programmes; rent for land, buildings and equipment; capital charges, and so on. At the same time, the flow of capital services can also be captured through indicators measuring such things as supplier and contractor payments; and the like. In addition to using the prices that are paid for endogenous inputs, volume-based input indicators associated with labour intensity include: the number of staff employed; the ratio of administrative to production staff (or administrative intensity); the number of hours worked by employees; the number of meetings held. Volume-based input indicators associated with capital intensity include: counts of the stock of hardware, buildings and equipment; the stock of software; the number of suppliers; the numbers of shared facilities.

In addition to incorporating the actual inputs used to produce public services when measuring productive efficiency, it is important to try to capture the under-utilization of resources, or slack, within the production system. Public organizations, like their private sector counterparts, actively store slack within their budgets – and may have good reasons for maintaining a 'rainy-day' fund that is not linked to future investment plans. However, the storing up of reserves can also be seen as an indicator of inefficiency, especially by political masters (Audit Commission 2012). For many public organizations, figures on unallocated reserves will be accounted for in the budgeting process, and so it is possible to build the level of slack directly into an efficiency analysis. For others, it may require some careful inspection of the costs and expenditure data.

Exogenous resource inputs

Measurement of the allocation of resources within public organizations is not without its challenges, but is generally more straightforward than the quantification of the external resources that are brought to bear upon public service production. Exogenous inputs in public services are essentially composed of the activities, capabilities and capacities of the individuals to whom services are provided. Within the public administration literature, these inputs are characterized as the coproduction of public services (Ruggerio 1996). Many public administration scholars conceptualize coproduction broadly, incorporating any action on the part of a citizen, no matter how small or seemingly insignificant (e.g. submitting a tax return), that could be regarded as an input into the service production process (Alford 2009). However, it is not always practical (let alone possible) to directly measure the extent of active involvement in the production of a public service, and so analysts tend to rely upon proxies for actual physical coproduction, such as education or population density (e.g. De Witte and Geys 2013). This, in turn, signals that what is usually measured is not coproduction *per se* but the potential for coproduction. The measurement of exogenous inputs can therefore reflect actual coproduction activities (e.g. number of hours of voluntary work within a school), coproduction capabilities (e.g. the percentage of the client population educated to high school level or better), or coproduction capacity (e.g. the community organizational life within an area).

The role that coproduction plays in public services is clearly one that must be incorporated within the analysis of productive efficiency, since those organizations benefiting from greater service coproduction may be able to economize on the internal resource inputs that are required to meet desired output levels. Yet, there are also other external resources that are valued by organizations, which are less easily included within the analytical process. For example, resource dependency theory highlights that it is possible to regard expressions of support or approval from key external stakeholders as a kind of input that can either legitimize or delegitimize an organization's production decisions (Pfeffer and Salancik 1978). This type of symbolic input may not have a direct effect on efficiency, but could condition the effects of labour inputs on outputs by motivating managers and staff to work more or less productively. The full range of possible exogenous inputs in public service production can be usefully conceptualized using a PESTEL (Political Economic Social Technological Environment and Legal) framework (Johnson, Scholes and Whittington 2008). This framework illustrates that, however important, it is not only client characteristics and institutional forces that shape the outputs of public service production, but also wider macro-economic, technological, environmental and legal processes over which organizations may have little direct control.

Outputs

Many analysts argue that the measurement of outputs is the most challenging aspect of evaluating productive efficiency in the public sector (e.g. Borge, Falch and Tovmo 2008; Simpson 2009). In the private sector, it is relatively straightforward to agree and measure financial or physical outputs and outcomes. Businesses buy and sell goods on the open market, and so it is comparatively easy to assign a monetary value that corresponds to the worth, or value-added (or lost), of any given output. By contrast, the measurement of outputs and outcomes in the public sector is characterized by a much higher degree of complexity. Firstly, public organizations are typically required to meet multiple and potentially conflicting organizational goals. As a result, it is rarely the case that the output of any given public service provider can be measured using a single indicator. Secondly, many of the outputs produced in the public sector are the outcome of joint production by more than one organization. For example, the number of children cared for by public authorities is likely to reflect the work of several different agencies. Thirdly, as a consequence of the publicness of public services, the desired level and quality of their output is judged by a diverse array of constituencies beyond as well as within the organization, such as taxpayers, staff and politicians (Boyne 2003). This has important implications for how much of a public service should be provided, and, more significantly, to what quality standard.

Despite the technical and political complexities that surround the measurement of public service outputs, there are key tangible elements of those outputs that all stakeholders are likely to value (if to varying degrees). The sheer volume of service, the speed and timeliness with which services are delivered, and the extent to which they meet established service standards are all important markers of public sector output. The capacity of public organizations to do this effectively, the quality of their management and customer service, and the commitment to continuous improvement are also organizational outputs, in which external stakeholders take a direct interest. Broadly speaking, the conceptualization, measurement and management of all these public service outputs can be differentiated through the use of indicators of output quantity and output quality. Essentially, output quantity signifies the volume of a service produced or delivered, while output quality signifies the extent to which the output that is being produced meets some criterion of speed, intensity or responsiveness to user needs.

Output quantity

The quantity of outputs produced by a public service is often measured using volume indicators akin to those used to measure public service inputs. Typical examples of indicators therefore include: the tonnes of waste collected; the number of bus journeys made; the number of pupils schooled; the number of operations performed; the number of sorties flown by jet fighters; the number of criminals arrested and so on. In each case, these indicators of output quantity capture the idea that a public service is actually producing or delivering a product. Even so, careful interpretation is required to determine whether more or less output represents a genuine improvement in organizational functioning. In making such interpretations it is important to take exogenous inputs into account to ensure that the scale of output is properly contextualized. For instance, a high number of arrests in a society with a low crime rate might represent some kind of overproduction (or output slack) within the system, while a low number of arrests in a society with a high crime rate would represent some kind of underproduction (or input slack).

Although volume indicators based on activity counts clearly capture what public organizations are doing, some activities do not necessarily fall so neatly under the output rather than the input banner, especially in terms of the time allocated to a particular task. For example, the number of hours of contact time for school pupils is a measure of the amount of schooling that students have received (i.e. an output), but is also a measure of the amount of resource that has been allocated to the production of schooling (i.e. an input). This indicates that there is a category of intermediate input/outputs, or processes, that are important components of the public service production system. Within the business literature, these processes are typically conceptualized and measured as *throughputs* in one way or another (Hedley 1998). In developing models and methods for measuring and evaluating productive efficiency, it is therefore important to incorporate the throughputs linking inputs to outputs. It is also important to recognize that the sheer amount of service produced is only an intermediate step towards the delivery of quality outputs, and can be the source of both positive and negative scale effects on that quality.

Output quality

Within the public sector, the quality of service output is in the eye of the beholder. Whether by measuring output quality against some yardstick of acceptable or optimum standards or through customer feedback processes, judgements about service quality are inevitably subjective and contestable. That said, there is no reason *prima facie* to suppose that such judgements will always be controversial. Few people would argue against the desirability of timely police responses to emergency calls or of a high level of service satisfaction amongst the vulnerable people cared for by social service providers, for example. Rather, it is the priority attached to different indicators of quality and the preferred level of performance that is subject to debate; something that is perhaps more accurately portrayed as a debate about what counts as effectiveness in public services (Boyne 2002b).

Economists have devoted a great deal of thought to how the quality of output produced by public services can be monetized, ranging from assessments of the prices paid for similar services in the private sector to the development of complicated shadow pricing formulae. However, these efforts to deal with the complexities of measuring output in the public sector are invariably beset with conceptual and empirical complications of their own (Simpson 2009). In many cases, it is comparatively straightforward and intuitive to measure the quality of public service outputs in a way that reflects citizens' experience of those outputs (e.g. the percentage of buses arriving on time; hospital mortality rates; the percentage of children passing high school examinations; the percentage of arrests resulting in convictions; and the time taken to respond to routine enquiries). An important advantage of developing indicators of this kind is that they offer a clear and transparent yardstick by which to judge the achievements of public services against both their own prior achievements and those of comparator organizations – something, which has been the ostensible purpose of the public service output ratings schemes that have been developed in many countries.

Output ratings

As noted above, the principal challenges in measuring public service outputs are the issues of: i) multiple outputs; ii) joint outputs; and, iii) competing and/

or conflicting goals. In measuring the output of a given public organization it is therefore likely to be necessary to: i) combine several indicators to try to capture the total aggregated quantity and quality of the output of an organization; ii) develop proxies for the relative contribution of each organization involved in joint production or, alternatively, lump together and 'double count' the contributions of the separate organizations, or even treat joint-working as a separate production line; and, finally, iii) attach weights to those areas of service production that are valued the most by key stakeholders. In fact, during the past couple of decades, policy-makers and analysts attempting to evaluate the performance of public services have devoted a great deal of attention to developing output ratings schemes that can capture some of this complexity (van Dooren, Bouckaert and Halligan 2010).

A good example of this phenomenon in action is the evolution of the performance management regime imposed upon English local authorities during the 1990s and 2000s, which began initially with the introduction of performance indicators for each separate function carried out by a local government. These indicators were subsequently incorporated within an aggregate measure of service quality (the Comprehensive Performance Assessment (CPA)) that weighted the performance of different service areas by the size of their budget. The methodology adopted to deliver the CPA resulted in the publication of a performance score or rating that encapsulated the overall state of the public services being received by local citizens. Output rating schemes, such as the CPA, are a useful means to convey important information to the public who may have little time or inclination to systematically analyse the production of the public services that they receive. They can also provide the kind of quantifiable information which managers and policy-makers can use to make organizational improvements.

Modelling productive efficiency

The conventional approach to evaluating productive efficiency in the public sector is to develop a linear model of the service production function, and to then use some form of non-parametric programming technique to calculate efficiency scores for a set of comparable public organizations. Typically, this entails the testing of a simple input–output model using Data Envelopment Analysis (DEA) and related techniques. In its more complex formulations, this has come to be associated with the so-called Input–Output–Outcome (IOO) model, which seeks to incorporate not only the quantity of outputs produced by public services, but also their quality as the final endpoint of the production process. This more complex formulation is usually evaluated using a two-stage analytical process, whereby input–output scores derived from DEA type techniques are regressed onto multiple exogenous and endogenous inputs. Key to these types of modelling is the availability of data that have been or can be collected in a consistent way by the multiple public services within a given policy field. Such data are increasingly common within the public sector. However, even with robust data, considerable conceptual and methodological complexities remain for the analyst seeking to accurately pin down just how efficiently a public service is being produced.

Public service organizations typically produce multiple outputs, joint outputs, and carry out activities whose value is contested. Attempting to accommodate all of this complexity within a single linear model is almost certainly impossible. Models for evaluating productive efficiency that incorporate a more complex pattern of inter-relationships between inputs, throughputs, outputs and perhaps outcomes could be constructed using Structural Equation Modelling or the introduction of interaction terms to conventional linear regression approaches. However, these modifications to the linear production function still provide a somewhat simplified view of the complicated nature of outcomes in the public sector. Thus, some observers have suggested that a balanced scorecard approach to understanding efficiency and effectiveness in services could prove a useful alternative to IOO models (Boyne 2002b).

The 'Balanced scorecard' was originally developed as a way of bringing together the perspectives of different stakeholders on the key performance indicators that matter to them (Kaplan and Norton 1996). The advantage of this approach is that it links objectives, initiatives and measures within a multi-dimensional framework that incorporates the perspectives of multiple stakeholders on organizational achievements (McAdam and Walker 2003). The criteria, weighting, and interpretation of efficiency gains and losses for any given organization are likely to vary amongst key stakeholders (Andrews, Boyne and Walker 2006). By combining the analysis of key input and output indicators and mapping these against the different goals of stakeholders within a balanced scorecard it may be possible to arrive at a more comprehensive assessment of productive efficiency than would be achieved through reliance on a simple IOO-type model. Moreover, the balanced scorecard approach can enable public services to identify areas of strength and weakness and to plan out their strategic priorities.

By way of illustration, Table 3.1 shows what a hypothetical (and abridged) balanced scorecard for productive efficiency in the provision of education

Table 3.1 Balanced scorecard for productive efficiency of education services

Management	*Production staff (teachers)*
Total expenditure	*Total hours worked*
Staff sickness absence	Professional development opportunities
Parental involvement	Pupil welfare
Service users (parents)	*Government*
Taxation payable	*Grant allocations*
Teacher quality	Staff turnover
Examination grades	School leadership/management

Note: Input indicators are italicised

services might look like. The scorecard offers an indication of how some of the ways in which stakeholders' perceptions of what matters might vary. For example, the input that matters most to managers could be the total expenditure, for teachers the hours of pupil contact time, for parents the amount of (local) taxation they pay, and for government the amount of grant allocated to a given educational body. In terms of outputs, internally, staff absence (managers), professional development opportunities (teachers), teacher quality (parents) and personnel stability (government) will be important; whereas externally, parental involvement (managers), pupil welfare (teachers), exam grades (parents) and school leadership (government) will count. In many, if not most, cases, the different stakeholder groups would be able to agree on a set of indicators, however, the degree of importance that they attach to a given indicator is still likely to differ.

Improving productive efficiency

Policies to promote productive efficiency have long been the object of government attention, especially in response to the expansion of social demands or the decline of economic fortunes. The evolution of efficiency-orientated policy ideas focused initially very much on the question of production economies, especially in terms of the scale, scope, and increasingly now, the flow of the functions undertaken by public service organizations. More recent attempts to improve the cost-effectiveness of public services have been associated with the rise of the New Public Management (NPM) and reforms intended to make public services (and servants) more business-like in one way or another. Thus, broadly speaking, there are two principal approaches to promoting the productive efficiency of public services: the first focuses on ascertaining an appropriate size, structure and process for delivering a service, and redesigning organizations in line with the resulting calculations; the second is concerned with creating the kinds of institutional arrangements that can motivate public managers to manage resources more effectively.

The first of the two approaches is based firmly in the economics of production; efficiencies are to be gained from producing services at the optimal scale, scope or flow. Reforms aimed at capturing production economies therefore tend to be concerned with merging smaller organizations into larger ones, producing multiple outputs from the same site and the use of process engineering techniques. By contrast, the second approach is based on the economics of incentives, and reflects arguments regarding the need to reorientate bureaucrats' budget-maximizing behaviour towards performance improvement and efficiency savings. Typical reforms are competition, cross-sectoral partnership, agencification and performance management. The relationship between the interventions intended to improve productive efficiency and public sector inputs and outputs is illustrated in Figure 3.1.

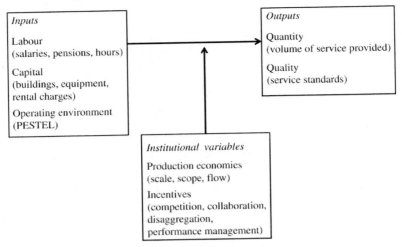

Figure 3.1 Modelling improvements in productive efficiency.

Production economies

The efficient production of public services is one of the most enduring questions in the study of public economics (Lomax 1943; 1952; Farrell 1957). At what level of input can public service organizations function most efficiently? Can those organizations benefit from economies of scale? How might they realize economies of scope? Is it possible to economize on the flow of service production? Questions about the potential for appropriately designed organizations to realize production economies go straight to the heart of public service production. As we have seen, that requires the application of myriad inputs to ensure that the production of desired outputs can be achieved. Hence, judgements about appropriate levels of output are inherently bound up in questions about the appropriate scale, scope and timing of production inputs. Answers to those questions cannot always be determined precisely in advance, given the many factors that must be controlled to attain the desired match between inputs and outputs. It is perhaps no surprise, therefore, that public managers and policy-makers, in particular, often prefer to adopt simple structural strategies for increasing the scale and scope of production to realize improvements in the input–output ratio of public services.

Economies of scale

Economies of scale occur when the average cost of each unit of input required to produce a unit of output is decreasing. Such costs tend to fall when organizations are able to produce more outputs with the same amount of inputs. Conventional economic arguments on scale effects for public services suggest that large public organizations accrue scale economies because they can spread fixed inputs (e.g. staff, technology, premises) across a wider range and higher quantity of outputs (Stigler 1958). This also often implies that scale economies are more readily found in the provision of capital rather than labour-intensive services, because the cost of fixed assets, such as waste disposal sites and water supply chains, remain stable through time and can be spread more easily across an increasing number of service recipients. By contrast, labour-intensive services, such as education or social care, require the kind of close contacts with clients, which are difficult to economize on in terms of the investment of time required to deliver a quality product – though it is possible to reduce labour costs through contracting out, new hiring practices, increased specialization or some form of de-professionalization.

For many public economists, scale economies tend to follow a relatively predictable pattern that culminates eventually in decreasing returns to scale as public organizations simply become too big to manage efficiently (Buchanan 1965; Tullock 1965; Williamson 1967). However, policies to promote productive efficiency rarely seek to identify the precise point at which scale economies might turn from positive to negative, and generally assume that 'bigger is better'. Amalgamations and mergers of public service organizations are frequently mandated in pursuit of scale economies; though in some countries, voluntary mergers between public organizations providing similar services are the norm, especially at the local level (Faulk and Hicks 2011). Often, such restructuring is undertaken with the goal of capturing administrative as well as production economies, since 'back-office' costs (e.g. senior management team, corporate services) are typically fixed and are therefore, in principle, spread more easily across a larger organization. Production efficiency gains may also result from the 'pecuniary gain' of lower input prices as a result of the greater purchasing power of big organizations (Shepherd 1990).

A large amount of research has investigated the presence of scale economies within local government (see Dollery, Grant and Kortt 2012 for a review), and in other labour-intensive services, especially schools (see Colegrave and Giles 2008 for a review) and universities (see Lewis and Dundar 1999 for a review). Scale economies in capital-intensive services such as transportation, water supply and waste management services are also a frequent topic of research (see Bel 2013 for a review). However, the study of scale economies in healthcare, social services and other areas of the public sector has somewhat lagged behind this research. The evidence from the reviews of the existing studies is generally mixed, but one theme that emerges is that there may be an optimum size after which economies of scale recede (Bel 2013; Colegrave and Giles 2008). A weakness in nearly all of the studies though is that they offer only observational accounts of the relationship between scale and costs, rather than an assessment of productive efficiency before and after structural changes.

Several studies of the impact of hospital mergers in the US suggest that they result in considerable cost-savings (e.g. Dranove and Lindrooth 2003; Spang, Arnould and Bazzoli 2009), though, of course, it is important to note that these studies incorporate for-profit as well as not-for-profit hospitals. The handful of studies that evaluate the impact of a planned change in the size of local governments offer contradictory findings. Gordon and Knight's (2008) assessment of the voluntary amalgamation of school districts in the State of Iowa during the 1990s suggests that very few of the anticipated efficiencies were realized, whereas Reingewertz's (2012) analysis of forced municipal amalgamations in Israel during 2003 suggests such reforms can lead to lower levels of expenditure and better fiscal health. More research of this nature in different settings would be valuable, especially given the predilection for structural change as a reform option and the sums of public money this often entails.

In recent times, 'hard' structural tools of reform have been supplemented with 'softer' approaches that seek to make public services work together in pursuit of scale. Indeed, if it is the scale of production that matters rather than the governance structure, in theory, economies of scale can be garnered just as effectively where one or more providers are required to produce outputs jointly, as when those providers are merged to increase the overall scale of the operation. At the same time as being directed to do so by their political masters, public services themselves can voluntarily seek out the kinds of joint production that policy-makers increasingly advocate (Ling 2002). Whether by better coordinating the work of the disparate public agencies across a given area or by pooling resources and expertise, joint production is thought to result in reduced total inputs and increased total output. However, evidence on the gains in productive efficiency from joint service production is extremely thin on the ground. Andrews and Entwistle's (2010) cross-sectional analysis indicates that local government departments in Wales that partner more intensively with other public services appear to garner gains in cost-effectiveness, but few other studies of joint production capture efficiency savings or losses.

In addition to externally-facing structural changes, public services can also implement internal changes in pursuit of scale economies. Firstly, it is possible to gain scale economies from supplying the same amount of a service to a larger number of customers. So, if we take the example of a teacher in a classroom, one might pack in additional students to realize scale economies. Secondly, economies of scale could be captured by cutting back on the labour or capital costs for a given service. For instance, the number of dustmen on a waste collection truck could be reduced. Although inferences about the relative merits of these approaches can be drawn from the analysis of efficient production frontiers (see Emrouznejad, Parker and Tavares 2008, for a review), few studies systematically evaluate deliberate strategies for realizing internal scale economies. Hugh-Jones' (forthcoming) analysis of the impact of budget cuts in the US public library system between 1993 and 2009 indicates that levels of productivity fell further than predicted, suggesting that internal restructuring activities may be as likely to damage efficiency as drive it upward.

Economies of scope

Public organizations typically deliver a whole variety of different public goods. They may therefore be particularly well-placed to realize economies of scope. Whereas economies of scale are accrued by increasing the output level for existing products, economies of scope are captured by expanding the line of different products whilst retaining the existing delivery system. Thus, scope economies occur where the cost of providing 'a diversified set of services is less than the cost of specialized firms providing those same services' (Grosskopf and Yaisawamg 1990: 61). The conventional source of economies of scope is via the 'sharing of some inputs in the production of related goods or services, where these shared inputs are also often fixed' (Grosskopf and Yaisawamg 1990: 61). By realizing such economies, organizations can reduce the financial burdens caused by administrative duplication and lower internal transaction costs across and between different sub-units. For public services, fixed inputs which can be shared include computing facilities, central administrative staff and decentralized area offices. If all the public services within a given area were to share some common overheads then the vertical integration of those costs would result in productive efficiency gains.

Strategies for the realization of scope economies are often handed down by higher levels of government. A good example of this is the introduction of capital charges on the property assets of local government (Heald and Dowdall 1999). At the same, the rationalization of their property and asset portfolio can be undertaken independently by any public organization seeking scope economies. Furthermore, those organizations can also carry out internal structural reforms that are designed to capture potential scope economies within bureaucracies. Two examples here include: first, the setting-up of cross-cutting departments that are responsible for different production units; and, second, the centralization of all the support services within the production units at the corporate centre of an organization. So, for example, a university seeking out scope economies might integrate the management of different academic schools within a smaller number of broad faculties, and also concentrate all of the human resource management, finance, and IT functions of individual departments within the vice-chancellor's (or president's) office at the heart of the institution. Other strategies for capturing scope economies that are now commonly adopted by public services include the use of one-stop shops for dealing with customer enquiries and complaints. Moreover, these types of centralization might also occur on a smaller scale within the departments of large professional bureaucracies.

To date, research on the relationship between indicators of production scope and the efficiency of public services has focused largely on capital-intensive services (see Bel 2013 for a review) and universities (Lewis and Dundar 1999), much of which uncovers the presence of scope economies, though in some cases diseconomies of scope are also observed (e.g. Agasisti and Johnes 2010). Even so, very few studies have systematically analysed the impact of changes in the scope of service provision on the ratio of inputs to outputs. Andrews' (2013) analysis of the impact of vertical consolidation in English county governments during the 2000s suggests that administrative scope economies can be obtained through structural changes, but not production economies. Studies in other settings and sectors would usefully add to this thin evidence base.

Economies of flow

Scale and scope economies are, to a large extent, supply-side efficiencies, the result of planned changes in levels of output or the distribution of outputs. Economies of flow, by contrast, are associated with demand-side efficiencies captured by tailoring services more closely to customer's actual requirements. Strategies for capturing economies of flow are therefore essentially concerned with achieving efficiencies in the process of service provision, particularly through the scheduling of production and delivery. Introducing management systems that can better map service production on to service demand, in particular, can have several positive efficiency-enhancing effects (Seddon 2008). First, it may lower the amount of excess capacity (or slack) within the production system, for example, by reducing the number of times a particular service needs to be delivered, thereby eliminating overproduction. Second, by bringing the front-line and back office into closer alignment, the costs of administering public services can be made more manageable. As such, flow economies may go hand in hand with technological improvements in the delivery of key services.

One of the key ways in which flow economies have been pursued in recent years is through the development of e-government systems. By facilitating service exchanges online, e-government can, in theory, enable public organizations to produce only as much of a service as is actively sought out by citizens, enhancing their ability to manage 'preventable demand' in a more efficient way. Other examples of the ways in which flow economies are captured by public services can be found in the field of waste collection. The replacement of weekly with fortnightly waste collection is an attempt to gain economies by changing the sequencing of a service – it also incorporates an attempt to shift some of the cost of service production onto the consumer, by requiring that they cut down on the waste they produce.

A handful of case studies of public organizations introducing process improvements have suggested that business re-engineering may hold the key to harnessing flow economies that contribute to productive efficiency (Middleton 2010; Radnor 2010). However, to date precious little empirical research has rigorously investigated the idea of flow economies in the public sector. While the application of techniques, such as Lean management, and its derivatives (e.g. Leagile, Six Sigma), is increasingly advocated by public management specialists (Radnor and Osborne 2013), there is no systematic evidence to back up the claims of either the supporters or detractors of the techniques of business process improvement.

The economics of incentives

One of the assumptions of the economics of production is that essentially management inputs remain the same whatever the scale, scope or flow of service production. However, since public services are often bound by statute to provide certain services, the opportunity for reconfiguring the ways in which a service is produced can be somewhat limited. This, in turn, can lead organizations to seek savings by reducing labour costs. Aside from simply making workers unemployed or reducing their wages or hours, it is possible that the ways in which people are managed can improve efficiency. Government efforts to improve management in the public sector have invariably embodied the belief that public officials are motivated by self-interest, which leads them to perform only those tasks that are absolutely necessary to the roles that they occupy. At the street-level, this can be seen as an inevitable by-product of the daily grind of work on the front-line (Lipsky 1980), but, in the administrative centre of public services it is frequently regarded as the result of a cynical desire to seek out the rents of public office (Niskanen 1971). As we have seen, public choice theories suggest that bureaucrats are inherently self-interested and that it is necessary to devise checks and balances that prevent them from extracting rents from holding office. From a similar perspective, principal– agent theories suggest that without appropriate monitoring systems senior management or policy-makers (the principals) are unable to control the activities of employees (the agents). To address this problem it is necessary to change the incentive structure for public employees, especially by exposing them to market forces and introducing performance management systems.

Competition and collaboration

The use of market mechanisms to inject competitive pressures into the public sector is one of the most striking features of the landscape of public administration during the past thirty years. Whether through the privatization or deregulation of public services (Swann 1988), compulsory competitive tendering processes or the establishment of internal markets (Eliassen and Sitter 2008), the forces of competition and contestability are thought to drive costs down by prompting service providers to set and pursue lower prices. The contestability effect is realized most clearly through a procurement process in which certain parts of a public service are subject to competitive contracting, especially where this is open to bids from private firms (Domberger and Jensen 1997).

Advocates of competitive tendering argue that it prompts providers to focus on improving the quality of the work and reducing the costs wherever possible – for fear that a failure to please their clients will lead to a loss of business (Savas 1987). In this vein it can be argued that it doesn't matter whether contracts are awarded to public or private suppliers since it is the process of competitive tendering which provides the drive for increased efficiency

(Hodge 1998). Hence, it seems reasonable to assume that public organizations which are positively disposed to private contractors, in particular, will be more likely to enjoy the benefits of contestability effects than those that are determined to protect public sector monopolies. Evidence from a range of research suggests that the involvement of the private sector in public service provision can reduce production costs (for reviews see Andrews, Boyne and Walker 2011; Domberger and Jensen 1997; cf. Bel, Fageda and Warner 2010). However, it may also lead to a deterioration of service quality due to high transaction costs and poor contract specification (e.g. Knapp *et al.* 1999; Amirkhanyan, Kim and Lambright 2008).

In addition to the introduction of contestable markets for public services, governments have devoted attention to devising systems that can mimic the effects of pricing information in a competitive market. This can range from the promotion of voluntary benchmarking schemes, such as those used by the European Union to prompt organizations to be more environmentally-friendly (e.g. EUAMAS), right the way through to the extensive school league tables used by the UK Department of Education to publicly name 'excellent' and 'poor' schools. These systems of 'benchmark' or 'yardstick' competition are intended to incentivize organizations to work more efficiently by informing potential service users about the quality of the product that they are receiving and to the alternatives that are on offer.

A growing number of studies furnish evidence of the beneficial effects of competition on output quality in healthcare (see Propper 2012, for a review). However, to date much less attention has been paid to the impact of competition on productive efficiency. Andrews' (2010) review of studies of the relationship between competition (market or benchmarked) and productive efficiency suggests that cost-savings are likely to be realized through the application of this form of market pressure. However, most of the studies included in that review did not apply a before and after research design. Gaynor, Moreno-Serra and Propper's (2010) difference-in-difference analysis of the effects of competition in the English NHS, and Lockwood and Porcelli's (2013) analysis of its effects in English local government suggest that the introduction of competition improved output performance but did not generate cost-savings. All of which, suggests there is a need for more research that seeks to capture the causal effects of competition.

In addition to seeking to mimic the competitive pressures of the free market, governments have attempted to draw upon the expertise of organizations outside the public sector in a number of different ways. At the individual level, this has taken the form of efforts to attract private and voluntary sector managers into the public sector, the promotion of business management training for public officials and also performance-related pay for professionals and executives. To date, researchers have not sought to test whether private sector managerial experience has had an efficiency pay-off for public services, though the actual motivation of sector-switchers has come under scrutiny (e.g. Boardman, Bozeman and Ponomariov 2010). A large number of studies have examined the motivational effects of different forms of performance-related pay (see Perry, Engbers and Jun 2009, for a partial review), with several uncovering positive effects on output quality (e.g. Atkinson *et al.* 2009), but few offering a systematic assessment of its effects on the costs of attaining that improvement.

At an organizational level, bringing know-how from beyond the public sector into the public services has involved a variety of initiatives intended to enable public services to learn best practices from business and the voluntary sector. In some cases, this has entailed the use of consultancy firms to advise public organizations, in others it has been accomplished through the development of strategic alliances and partnerships between public, private and also voluntary sector organizations. Partnerships with the private sector are hypothesized to deliver improved technical efficiency by unlocking new finances for investment or, critically, gaining knowledge spillovers (Osborne and Gaebler 1992). Similar arguments apply to the involvement of the not-for-profit, third or voluntary sector in the provision of public services, though nonprofit and voluntary organizations also have particular strengths in client knowledge that can be harnessed by public sector partners in the pursuit of innovative ways to make efficiency savings.

Despite the existence of a massive literature on the relationship between privatization and efficiency (Hodge 2000), and growing evidence on the costs of public–private partnership (especially Private Finance Initiatives – see, for example, Pollock, Price and Player 2007), few studies provide a systematic analysis of the connection between such partnership and efficiency. Amongst those that do, Andrews and Entwistle (2010) find that partnership with the private sector and with the nonprofit sector has no relationship with the productive efficiency of local government departments in Wales.

Disaggregation and agencification

While most of the incentive-orientated initiatives discussed thus far are intended to exert indirect pressure on public officials or to introduce new ideas into public service organizations, it is also the case that more systematic structural changes are sometimes seen as the most effective way to induce efficiency-orientated behaviour. Public choice theorists devoted a great deal of attention to illustrating the virtues of disaggregation within the local government system. According to them, small local governments have to compete for fiscally mobile residents, and one of the ways in which they will do this is by competing on tax 'prices' for local services (e.g. Salmon 1987). On this reading, rather than pursuing economies of scale though consolidation and amalgamation, policy-makers would do better to encourage disaggregation and fragmentation. This, in turn, would prompt public organizations and managers to improve their strategic and operational management in order to stay competitive. In fact, this prescription for making public services more manageable has underpinned the development of arm's-length agencies and corporations to deliver services free of direct political control at both the local and central levels.

Through the devolution of power to lower levels of government and the establishment of single-purpose agencies for service delivery, agencification and corporatization is assumed to give managers greater control over budgets. Budget autonomy, in turn, is thought to empower managers to cut costs. According to the budgeting theories, where managers participate more actively in organizational decisions, they arguably have less need to behave defensively and hoard slack resources (Cammann 1976; Schein 1979). Similarly, separation of the purchasing and providing arms of public organizations is thought to enable purchasing managers to drive the price of service delivery downwards by giving them greater responsibility for doing their job as effectively as possible (Hood 1991). All of these reforms have accorded managers greater freedom to deliver in whatever way they deem necessary to achieve results, but have they had the desired effects on the productive efficiency of public services?

A number of studies have examined the relationship between some form of agencification and efficiency. Bilodeau *et al.* (2007) find that corporatization, through the designation as a special operating agency or autonomous service agency, of 11 Canadian federal agencies resulted in improvements in employee productivity, though not for overall cost-efficiency measured as unit of output per cost of input. By contrast, disaggregation of local authority services in England and Wales by breaking up the responsibilities for key functions into smaller geographical units is found by Boyne (1996) to be associated with worse waste management efficiency. Ferrari (2006), however, indicates that the establishment of a purchaser–provider split had no detectable effect on the efficiency of Scottish hospitals. By contrast, Gonzalez and Trujillo (2008) provide evidence of a small statistically significant improvement in productive efficiency in the wake of the decentralization of further powers to Spanish port authorities. Lee *et al.* (2008), too, find that the efficiency of Korean hospitals improved as a result of reforms encouraging specialization. Söderlund *et al.* (1997) suggest that both the introduction of purchaser–provider split and the resulting increase in purchaser power have enhanced efficiency in English hospitals.

Performance management and monitoring

Whereas competition, disaggregation and agencification are intended to devolve control to the managers responsible for public services, other elements of the economics of incentives are more closely aligned with a desire to increase central control over public officials. In particular, the political imperatives behind the pursuit of better quality services at a lower cost, have led to an emphasis on output controls and performance monitoring, with measured achievements being linked to resource allocation and rewards (Hood 1991). Central to making this process a success has been the application of performance management practices similar to those found in the private sector, such as Total Quality Management (Boyne *et al.* 2002). In many cases, such systems have been mandated by government (e.g. Best Value in the UK), but in others they form part of a wider cultural change brought about by NPM pressures (e.g. Managing for Results in US state governments). In theory, effective performance information systems enable managers to formulate, implement and monitor organizational goals. Thompson (2002), for example, suggests that for public services measurement and control systems are especially important because they enable managers (and politicians) to review and analyse the resources spent and results achieved.

Despite the massive amount of attention devoted to performance management in the public administration literature (Van Dooren, Bouckaert and Halligan 2010), surprisingly little research has systematically analysed the impact of performance management systems on performance itself (Boyne 2010a). A small number of cross-sectional studies address the relationship between performance management systems and productive efficiency. Macinati (2008) uncovers no efficiency gains resulting from the use of new management information systems by Italian healthcare providers, while Schubert (2009) finds that performance evaluation systems are largely unrelated to the efficiency of German university research units. Andrews and Van de Walle (2013), by contrast, uncover a strong relationship between the use of performance management in English local governments and citizens' perceptions of efficiency. Again, this critical issue in the management of public service efficiency would benefit from further research. Before and after studies of the impact of target-setting on public service outcomes identify positive effects on output quality (Boyne and Chen 2007; Kelman and Friedman 2009), so extending this type of work to the issue of productive efficiency would be especially valuable.

Conclusion

This chapter began with a discussion of the nature of productive efficiency in public services. The inescapable salience of questions about the ratio between inputs and outputs was discussed. Following that, the inputs and outputs that might be taken into consideration within an efficiency analysis were outlined, before the potential value of a balanced scorecard for delivering judgements about productive efficiency was considered. Thereafter, the chapter elaborated on the theoretical underpinnings and practical recommendations of two key approaches to improving the productive efficiency of public services: the first dealing with the economics of production; the second concerned with the economics of incentives. The merits of these alternative approaches to improving productive efficiency were evaluated through a selective reading of key empirical studies. Three key themes emerge from our examination of productive efficiency in public services.

First, the conceptualization of the productive efficiency of public services is inevitably bound up in its operationalization and measurement. For that reason, concepts and indicators of productive efficiency (like those of all the other dimensions of public service efficiency) are inherently political in nature. A balanced scorecard approach to evaluating productive efficiency offers the potential for bringing together a wide range of perspectives on its improvement in a way that is useful for politicians, public managers and citizens. Second, even though public managers and organizations have now evolved to embrace inter-organizational as well as intra-organizational management, the rationales advanced for efficiency-orientated innovations remain grounded in either the economic language of production or incentives. Although there is growing openness to alternative approaches to efficiency improvement, such as Lean management and cross-sectoral partnership, these notions remain rooted in established economic theories, which signal the challenge of envisaging new answers to the productive efficiency problem. Third, the evidence on the relative merits of alternative strategies for improving efficiency suggests that it is possible to capture gains in productive efficiency, but that those gains may be highly dependent upon the type of strategy for improving efficiency that is implemented. For example, the findings from the literature on production economies offer few hard and fast rules for the pursuit of efficiency gains, whereas those from the research on incentives suggest that competition and disaggregation, in particular, may offer the surest prospect of success.

The discussion of productive efficiency offered in this chapter serves as the foundation for the exploration of the measurement and management of the other faces of service efficiency that we identify as core to the work of public managers and organizations. We turn next to distributive efficiency, which captures the idea that some criterion of social equity should be applied to the provision of public services. In fact, one might regard this as the most political dimension of public service efficiency, since it deals with questions of social as well as economic efficiency.

4 Distributive efficiency

In the previous chapter, we laid out why and how public services are driven to maximize outputs over inputs. We also explored the ways in which policy-makers and managers typically attempt to achieve improvements in the inputs required to achieve desired levels of service quantity and quality. We argued that decisions about productive efficiency are an inescapable feature of public policy and administration because of the constrained budgets which characterize public service provision. Still, the technocratic foundations of productive efficiency render it something of a servant of the other dimensions within the public service efficiency lexicon, which tend to be shaped to a greater extent by democratic and social considerations. In particular, questions within government about how to best create social value or to build a good society inevitably give rise to decisions about the distribution of public services between the different groups within society.

Productive efficiency is enhanced where the cost implications of providing high-quality services at the right volume are minimized. Although this dimension of efficiency can highlight whether the services provided by public organizations are, on average, cost-effective, it does not necessarily tell one much about how fairly those services are distributed to the people whose need is greatest. In fact, society as a whole may benefit less from the provision of a standard package of services, which fails to take into account the distinctive needs or capabilities of some individuals or groups of individuals. Technical decisions about the best way to organize a particular service are not attuned to actual or perceived inequities in the provision of services. They are concerned, above all, with standardization. There are, however, many political, institutional and managerial factors that might explain why the provision of public services is experienced differently by the various social groups within a given user population.

From a political point of view, the policy agenda of ruling political parties is likely to matter. So, for example, it might be the case that a party is elected to office with a mandate to increase public expenditure on schools, but this, of course, does not benefit those taxpayers who do not have children or who choose to educate their children privately. From an institutional point of view, the capacity of public services to address the needs of different social groups may have important implications for how citizens perceive service equity. For instance, a commitment to providing welfare services to immigrants may require that some resources are diverted from meeting the existing population's needs. From a managerial point of view, it is likely that the values of bureaucrats shape the service experiences of citizens. Lipsky (1980) and Maynard-Moody and Musheno (2000) illustrate how street-level bureaucrats make decisions about the effort they dedicate to helping clients on the basis of subjective judgements of deservingness. Moreover, the literature on representative bureaucracy highlights that public sector managers and professionals often seek to advance the interests of the social groups from which they are drawn (Peters, Schröter and Von Maravic 2012). Thus, as well as deciding to what standard of quality services should be produced and the quantity of services to be produced, the state is also responsible for deciding for whom services should be provided and the acceptable cost of distributing services on the basis of some criterion of fairness or equity.

In examining the nature of distributive efficiency in the public sector, we draw upon economic theory and political philosophy to explore what fairness and equity mean when applied to the distribution of goods and services by public organizations. We consider how distributive efficiency and its costs can be measured and then reflect upon the main ways in which government has sought to alter the distribution of public services, the motivation behind such distributional policies and their financial implications. The chapter opens with a discussion of the limitations of Pareto efficiency as a guiding principle for the pursuit of distributive efficiency in public services, reflecting upon alternative approaches to thinking about fairness and equity in the public sector. Thereafter, the measurement and evaluation of distributive efficiency is examined, before we review evidence on the impact of policies for its promotion and draw conclusions about the varying approaches to distribute public services more efficiently.

What is distributive efficiency?

The question of distributive efficiency is at the heart of the study of public economics (Hindricks and Myles 2006; Stiglitz 2000). According to conventional economic theory, efficiency and equity are in a state of perpetual tension, and it is usually by trading one off against the other that improvements in either can be attained (Wolf 1987). Within this setting, it is the work of Vilfredo Pareto that still dominates debates about distributive efficiency. Put simply, according to Pareto, a distribution of goods or services may be characterized as optimally efficient where any alterations in that distribution to make some group or individual better off have the consequence of making another group or individual worse off. However, this notion is not without its problems. In particular, when determining Pareto optimality, the criteria for evaluating distributive efficiency tend to be shaped more by questions of efficiency than distributional questions (Wolf 1987). Yet, in the real world of public policy and administration, distributional issues often trump those of efficiency (Viner 1960). The theoretical demands of Pareto efficiency too may not stack up.

Pareto optimality does not necessarily result in a socially desirable or just distribution of resources, since the utility of each group or individual is taken to be equivalent and it is therefore all but impossible for redistribution not to harm someone's utility. For some economists, this confirms that government must not intervene in the workings of the free market (e.g. Arrow and Debreu 1954). For another group, it suggests that the requirements of Pareto optimality be modified to incorporate compensation for people made worse off through redistribution (Hicks 1939; Kaldor 1939). Yet, for others it highlights serious problems with the assumptions that underpin Paretian economics, especially its reliance on the doctrine of perfect competition (Greenwald and Stiglitz 1986), and its crude conception of utility (Self 1985).

Lerner (1944) persuasively argues that a Pareto-efficient distribution of resources is beset by the problem of diminishing marginal utility. That is, a unit increase in the resources of a wealthy person actually constitutes a much lower return to utility than the same unit increase for a poor person, for whom even small resource-gains may represent a much larger rise in marginal utility. For Lerner, society itself stands to gain from the redistribution of (some) resources from the wealthy to the least-advantaged. Not only does social justice demand some form of wealth redistribution on the grounds of what is right, but improvements in social efficiency are achieved through redistribution to the poor. There is therefore, *prima facie*, good reason for anticipating that government will play a key role in ensuring that the distribution of resources is equitable enough to maximize social efficiency.

All of this highlights that broadly speaking, distributive efficiency can be defined as the most efficient and effective process through which goods and services can be distributed to those in greatest need of them (Lerner 1944). Determining need means, however, that decisions about the distribution of public services are value-laden, causing notions of distributive efficiency to be as much a matter of political theory as (welfare) economics. In fact, several scholars have sought to integrate principles of distributive justice (such as the difference principle advanced by John Rawls (1972)) with conventional economic theory to develop normative arguments for the efficiency of a social contract, which requires redistributive public policies (e.g. Swygert and Yanes 1998; Mercier Ythier 2010).

By incorporating questions of inequity and fairness within the public service efficiency equation, the concept of distributive efficiency, following Rawls, enjoins that the distributive effects of policy change must be to the benefit of the least-advantaged in society (Laslier and Picard 2002). Even so, many hard questions about distributive efficiency in public services still remain. In particular, we argue that the management of efficiency requires that distributional inputs and outputs be measured and that the impact of initiatives for the enhancement of distributive efficiency be analysed and evaluated. Given that this dimension of efficiency has a robust normative foundation, it is extremely important to be careful about the justification for the use of one measure of distributive efficiency rather than another.

Measuring the distributive efficiency of public services

More than productive efficiency, which can, to a certain degree, be reduced to the counting up of the number of units produced and gauging the quality of those units of output against some predefined standard, the specification of measures of distributive efficiency is at all points a normative exercise. By and large, questions about the fairness of the distribution of public services are highly subjective ones that depend upon the perceptions of the multiple stake-holders within the public service production system and upon the political beliefs that lie behind those perceptions. So, as for the question of productive efficiency, the views of public service stakeholders about the fairness with which services are distributed play an extraordinarily important role. However, politicians, managers, professionals and (especially) citizens, are much more likely to have divergent views about the nature of distributional equity and the extent to which it should be pursued, and at what cost.

The looming subjective element within questions of distributive efficiency might seem to imply that only measures that tap the perceptions of different stakeholders matter. Yet, even though the profoundly normative nature of distributive efficiency means that it is more highly contested than the other faces of public service efficiency, there are ways in which it can be measured that do not rely on the attitudes of relevant actors. Typically, the attempt to move away from subjective measurement of distributional issues involves efforts to disaggregate the quantity and quality of service outputs by different social groups. However, it can also be attained through the use of indicators designed specifically for the purpose of measuring distributional policy outcomes. Such output equity indicators are not just used to evaluate the achievement of policy goals, but can be used by pressure groups to hold governments accountable on distributional issues. In addition, data on the distribution of standard public service outputs can be used to gauge the extent to which service outputs are provided in a fair or equitable way. In general, each of these approaches begins with an effort to define which social groups are, or have been, disfavoured by the existing distribution of services, and to then calculate the extent to which that disadvantage is being overcome and at what cost.

Defining the target group

The measurement and management of public service equity is first of all determined by the theory of distributional equity that is being applied. A commitment to equality of opportunity for example, will mean that the dis-tributive efficiency of public services should be assessed in terms of the equality of access to services. By contrast, a commitment to equality of outcome should be assessed by examining to what extent certain social groups seem to be getting better or worse quality service outputs (i.e. output equity). In theory, both viewpoints can be incorporated within a Rawlsian perspective on social justice. In practice too, it is likely that equality of opportunity and outcome will be important considerations within the design and implementation of public management reforms, if to varying degrees.

These two broad approaches to equity presuppose different sorts of measurement for effective policy evaluation, especially a commitment to positive discrimination to right historic wrongs, which examines rates of change in equality of access and output equity, under the guise of fair treatment. In fact, each of these standards of distributional equity are key to understanding the ways in which the public sector is organized and run, as well as the types of public policies that are introduced to improve distributive efficiency.

Equality of access is in many respects a central feature of the justification for state provision of services. Theories of market failure suggest that one reason for the state's existence is its capacity to ensure that all citizens have access to public and social goods, such as education, culture and leisure, irrespective of the ability to pay (Stiglitz 2000). At the same time, a key principle underpinning the Weberian rationale for public bureaucracies is that the legal–rational basis of the state requires that it treat all citizens, clients or service users in exactly the same impersonal way, both in terms of access to services and the distribution of those services (Du Gay 2000). This notion of equal treatment is captured by the idea of procedural justice, and is a particular characteristic of the public philosophy of many modern democratic states, especially France where distinctions between citizens are not officially recognized (Favell 2001). At the same time, questions of distributional equity are rarely shaped solely by a commitment to procedural justice, but also rely very heavily on ideas about distributive justice, such as those advanced by John Rawls. Crucially, the demands of distributive justice can be interpreted as meaning that less-advantaged social groups should receive preferential treatment to overcome historic patterns of disadvantage (Ackerman 1980). Thus, equality of outcome is as much a legitimate policy goal as equality of opportunity.

Whatever the normative commitments underpinning ideas about distributional equity, the analytical demands for its evaluation have one important shared feature; that is, that it is necessary to develop some means of measuring and categorizing different social groupings. Only by developing such a categorization can the analyst determine whether all social groups are indeed receiving equal access to services, being treated fairly or receiving the kind of preferential treatment that helps to overcome socio-economic disadvantage. The social categories that matter for distributive efficiency in the public services are typically those that reflect the politics and society within any given state. A good real-world example of some of the most relevant social groups in this regard would be the protected categories within the UK Equality Act of 2010:

age, disability, gender reassignment, marriage and civil partnership, race, religion or belief, sex, and sexual orientation.

Subjective measures of distributional equity

Subjective survey-based measures are an important means for gauging citizens' and policy-makers' perceptions of distributional equity. In the previous chapter dealing with productive efficiency, we noted that such measures can be used to capture public views towards public service quality. Assessing whether those attitudes vary across social groups is an important step in gaining an understanding of the distribution of service quality across different groups. At the same time, questions about the ease of access to services and citizens' experiences when using public services could be added to surveys incorporating batteries of questions dealing with service quality. Surveys of public officials could also be used to assess how well they felt their organization was doing in making services accessible to different social groups, treating those groups fairly and so on. Aside from the value gained from simply gauging the views of citizens and officials on questions of equity, efforts to bring those contrasting viewpoints together could potentially reveal much about the gaps between rhetoric and reality that often characterize debates about distributional equity (Gay 2007).

In terms of specific survey items to capture citizens' perceptions of distributional equity, important areas of specific focus would include: the extent to which people are aware of the services to which they are entitled; the extent to which they use those services; whether or not they felt they had been discriminated against by public officials; or if they believed some particular groups were receiving unfair advantages through their dealings with the public sector. Of course, people's responses to these questions are likely to be susceptible to all kinds of prejudices and subjective biases. Evaluations of distributive efficiency must therefore be careful to take potentially damaging influences on citizens' perceptions of equity and fairness into account when seeking to examine the effects of changes in patterns of service production on distributional equity. Incorporation of the individual characteristics of respondents to service user surveys within models and/or the description of those characteristics and their potential impact is an important consideration; so too for data from surveys of public officials.

Items for inclusion in surveys of bureaucrats could be designed to mirror those asked of recipients of the services that they provide. So, for example, officials could be asked whether people were aware of the services to which they are entitled; whether people were using those services and so on. These matched questions could then be supplemented with a whole series of items dealing solely with officials' perceptions of the commitment to distributive efficiency within their own organization. This might run from questions asking whether the respondent's organization has a policy on fair treatment of service users and includes issues of equal treatment in codes of employee conduct, right through to questions asking if staff positively (or negatively) discriminate in favours of (or against) certain social groups. Respondents could find these latter questions difficult to answer in an open and honest way, and so guarantees of confidentiality are extremely important.

Objective measures of distributional equity

Subjective measures of equity within the public sector capture the idea that what people regard as fair matters when thinking about the distribution of services. In this respect, they offer a simple connection with the democratic legitimacy of public services and the limits to what can or cannot be pursued in the name of distributive efficiency. Notwithstanding the democratic value of subjective measures of equity, there are important aspects of distributional equity that might be better evaluated using objective indicators, which distinguish between the quantity and quality of outputs being provided to different social groups. In fact much of the existing research on equity within the public sector draws upon measures such as these. For example, the voluminous studies on equity in educational outcomes deal with variations between boys and girls, different social classes and different ethnic groupings within public school systems (for reviews of some of this work see Kao and Thompson 2003; Sirin 2005). And these kinds of measures have also been used by public administration researchers interested in the distributional effects of different managerial strategies and behaviours (e.g. O'Toole and Meier 2004b).

All of the objective output and outcome indicators described in chapter three can be drawn upon to analyse distributional equity provided they can be classified according to some criteria of social grouping. In addition to applying such classification to existing data, bespoke indicators can be devised that capture the impact of policies designed to promote distributional equity. Good examples of these kinds of indicators would include those that gauge the coverage of specific distributional initiatives (e.g. the proportion of government buildings that are accessible to disabled people; or the availability of HIV advisory services), and those that largely pertain to certain social groups (e.g. the number of domestic violence arrests; or the rate of reoffending amongst people on remand). When supplemented with data on the distribution of core outputs across key groups of interest and relevant input data, bespoke equity indicators can provide the kind of clear information required to underpin evaluations of distributive efficiency. Taken together, such indicators can enable policy-makers and public managers to identify areas of distributional equity in which public services are doing well and areas in which more or less resources might be needed.

Calculating the cost of distributional equity

Evaluations of distributive efficiency can draw upon the kinds of broad input indicators applicable to the evaluation of productive efficiency. However, measures that distinguish between the perceptions of service equity of different social groups would be better matched to input indicators that capture the actual amounts of time and money that were expended on serving those groups. While it is not likely or practical that such indicators be developed in every case of distributional equity, there are nonetheless many areas in which the construction of bespoke input indicators would prove highly valuable.

Input indicators that tapped how much resource was used with the specific aim of making improvements in distributional equity could be applied in at least three ways in the evaluation of distributive efficiency. First, the amount of time and money invested in achieving a desired change in the perceptions of the pattern of distribution of services between different groups could be calculated as a ratio or as a per capita figure. For example, the amount of additional contact time that teachers devote to improving the learning of students from disadvantaged backgrounds or from minority ethnic groups could be set against the resulting changes in the performance of those students.

Second, it would also be useful to calculate a ratio or percentage figure that indicated how much more-advantaged groups were made worse off compared to the gains in equity experienced by the groups targeted for redistributive interventions. This is akin to testing for Pareto efficiency, but needn't mean that the emergence of a large distributional gap is either intrinsically right or wrong when thinking about distributive efficiency. For example, the diversion of time spent teaching white, middle class students to assisting poor minority ethnic ones may be regarded as equitable, especially if resources are scarce and already advantaged students may possess a compensating home environment. Justification of such decisions is of course the very essence of the politics of distributive efficiency to which we will return in more detail in chapter seven.

Third, efforts to enhance distributional equity do not always result in a zero-sum game, in which one or more social groups suffers for improvements in the distribution of services to another social group. In some cases, public services could simply take particular care to ensure that they convince the members of different social groups that they are all being treated fairly – even if differently (Berman 1997). Alternatively, policy-makers and public managers might devote more time and resources to developing innovative new solutions to key distributional questions rather than simply redistributing resources from one group to another, thereby demonstrating their capacity for delivering distributively efficient services.

One further aspect of the costs associated with distributive efficiency is the potential for the displacement of organizational activities to occur. We noted above that distributional initiatives may mean that input intensity varies across different social groups, or that resources are diverted from existing to new areas of organizational activity. Measurement of how much resource is being diverted from other areas of organizational activity to meet the costs associated with policies to improve distributional equity is therefore something else that could be added to the assessment of the input demands of those policies.

Improving distributive efficiency

Public policies designed to improve patterns of distributional equity have become a central feature of government activity during the post-war period. Such policies are varied and numerous, and have usually emerged in response to the articulation of political demands to correct for gaps in income, status or power caused by perceived or real market failures. Whether it is political parties, pressure groups or social movements that are the source of demands for distributive justice, government and other nonmarket institutions are regarded as the agents best placed to meet those demands. In fact, such institutions also actively seek to shape and steer changes in the distribution of social and economic outcomes. Both the state and the not-for-profit sector devote much independent thought and energy to the design and development of distributional policies. The question of the efficiency of those policies is a perennial one, of course, given the limited resources of the organizations responsible for their delivery.

In the public sector, ideas about distributional policies are typically associated with large-scale social and political programmes, rather than narrow economic or managerial ones. So, for example, the notion of distributive justice is frequently invoked in defence of the welfare state (Arts and Gelisson 2001), but has rarely featured publicly in the NPM-inspired reforms of government and the public services. However, although the distributional consequences of NPM were not a key driver of its policy prescriptions, there are several ways in which policies characteristic of such reforms might be given a distributive twist (Harrow 2002). Consumerism within public services can have distributional benefits by improving equality of access and consistency in the treatment of service users (Pollitt 1988). Moreover, competition and choice mechanisms might enhance equality of opportunity by placing greater pressure on public services to be responsive to customer demand (Le Grand 2006). All the same, in general, core NPM initiatives are regarded as having negative distributional effects, largely because they prioritize the cost-cutting element of productive efficiency (e.g. worse service quality and equity (contracting out); 'cream-skimming' (competition); and freedom from effective oversight (agencification)).

In more recent times, network forms of public governance have been touted as having positive distributional effects because the way in which they bring together multiple stakeholder groups is more open and inclusive (Stoker 2006). However, such networks can often have a dark side, whereby public managers become co-opted into the political priorities of powerful stakeholders (O'Toole and Meier 2004b), and it is not clear that such network forms of organizing are designed with equitable outcomes in mind. In fact, we would argue that, in general, bureaucratic approaches to managing the public sector are most likely to be in tune with a distributive social or political programme – though of course they are also often associated with a concern for the productive efficiency of services. Bureaucratic means to achieving improvements in distributional equity typically take one of three forms.

First, at the macro level, distributional concerns are pursued through tax and spend policies. Although these kinds of policies can also be addressed at subnational levels of government, in most countries, central and federal governments set the agenda for large-scale distributional policies. Second, at the meso level, public organizations and managers may decide to change their priorities about those client groups they believe to be most deserving of additional support. This usually entails that existing resources are targeted at specific individuals, households or areas. Finally, at the micro level, regulatory regimes may be introduced that seek to change the behaviour of managers and professionals. Service standards set out in law or voluntary accreditation schemes that seek to promote best practice in advancing the interest of disadvantaged social groups are often developed with distributional goals in mind. The relationship between the interventions intended to improve distributive efficiency and public sector inputs and outputs is illustrated in Figure 4.1.

Tax and spend

For the general public, the media, politicians and political parties, ideas about distributional equity generally mean those macro-level economic policies that result in the transfer of income from one social group to another. Based on the assumption that distributive questions are generally guided by the idea that policy change should benefit the least-advantaged, this typically implies that high-income social groups are taxed more in order to fund public services and social programmes that will benefit lower-income groups (Daly 1992). Such tax-and-transfer policies are developed and implemented at multiple levels of government, and vary in scope and impact depending upon the

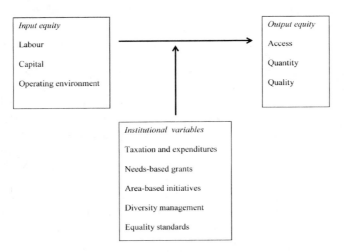

Figure 4.1 Modelling improvements in distributive efficiency.

relative degree of freedom each level of government has to raise tax revenue and redistribute the proceeds. In regionalized unitary states like France, Spain and the UK, this typically means that central government takes responsibility for most taxation and welfare provision. In federal states, such as Australia, Germany and the United States, the power to tax and transfer is more evenly spread between the federal and state governments, while in some more decentralized countries, such as Switzerland, local governments too have wide-ranging revenue-raising powers and autonomy over the redistribution of tax.

All taxation is undertaken with the aim of underwriting the activities of government, and so inevitably has distributional implications whether or not it is diverted directly to lower-income or less-advantaged groups through welfare payments. Governments vary taxation levels for different social groups on the basis of several criteria, including the ability to pay. Welfare payments, or packages, in many countries are also set at a differing level according to the needs of certain people. All of which requires ruling political parties to make and justify decisions about the distributive efficiency of one pattern of tax and transfer over another. Here, the links with allocative efficiency are often also apparent, with tax-and-transfer decisions frequently determined on the basis of political calculations about electoral preferences. At the same time, the raising of government revenue is necessary for the production of public services, and so the ways in which tax revenue is allocated to different policy areas at the macro-level represents a clear signal about the distributional priorities of any given government.

The relationship between alternative government taxation and spending patterns on distributional outcomes has been studied at the country and state government levels. Although most of this research is focused on the impact of inequality on government spending (e.g. Iversen 2005; Moene and Wallerstein 2003), a number of studies are concerned with the impact of government spending on inequality. Within this literature, Barrilleaux and Davis' (2003) finding that US states that spend more and tax more actually have higher levels of income inequality, seems to be atypical. Xu (2006), for example, finds that high levels of healthcare spending were associated with fewer health inequalities in the US states. Likewise, Wolff and Zacharias' (2007) analysis of income inequality across US households suggests that net government expenditure reduces inequality – though tax rates make no difference. At the local level in Norway, Aaberge, Bhuller, Langorgen and Mogstad (2010) find that targeted expenditure reduces income inequality in general, as well as for specific disadvantaged groups. A similar finding emerges from Evandrou *et al.*'s (1993) evaluation of taxation and spending in the UK. In fact, Roine, Vlachos and Waldenstrom's (2009) study of 16 major countries through the entire twentieth century suggests that high public expenditure and taxation reduces the share of national wealth held by top earners relative to those at the bottom of the pile.

In addition to making decisions about the distribution of revenue raised by standard income taxes, property taxes and taxes on goods and services, there are several kinds of specific taxation policies that may be implemented with a view to raising monies specifically for the enhancement of distributive efficiency. For instance, windfall taxes on bankers' bonuses might be introduced to underpin the funding of employment programmes for citizens in those regions hardest hit by the recent global recession. Similarly, so-called 'stealth taxes' might be used in times of economic liberalization to facilitate a transfer of resources from the wealthy to the least-advantaged either by targeting assets other than earned income or by subsidizing tax breaks for the poor (Newman 2003). Good examples of this kind of tax would be the levies imposed upon company cars or pension funds, or tax credits for low-income workers or single parents.

Stealth taxes are intended to increase the effective marginal tax rate for wealthier citizens. However, they can also be used in ways that effectively appropriate additional funds from less-advantaged groups, through such things as state-run lotteries or taxation on tobacco and alcohol consumption (Sowels 2011), and thereby have negative distributional consequences (at least, in the short term) for those groups with the greatest need. Although there is practically no systematic research on the operation of stealth taxes, what little work there is actually suggests they may not improve distributive efficiency. MacNaughton, Matthews and Pittman (1998) find that Canadian and US citizens on lower statutory tax rates are more likely to experience an inflated effective marginal tax rate courtesy of stealth taxes. Similarly, Freund and Morris (2005) uncover a connection between the use of state lotteries and income inequality in the US states.

Governments make choices about the distributional effects on taxpayers, as well as about how the resulting revenue should be redistributed. Thus, in practice, taxes are either progressive (that is, increase as the ability to pay increases); regressive (that is, increase as the ability to pay decreases); or proportional (that is, a fixed standard rate irrespective of the ability to pay). At the same time as varying the balance between progressive and regressive taxation in a bid to enhance distributive efficiency, government can also introduce charges for its services in ways that have distributional implications. For example, in developed countries, users can be charged fees for using leisure or transportation services, and these fees might be varied or subsidized for some social groups (e.g. older or unemployed people). In developing countries, this practice might be extended to access to public education or health services.

There are numerous analyses of the distributional inequity associated with user fees for medical services in both rich (Gemmill, Thomson and Mossialos 2008) and poor countries (Whitehead, Dahlgren and Evans 2001). Likewise, a growing empirical literature investigates the relationship between road user charging to achieve environmental goals and distributional equity (e.g. Mitchell 2005). However, comparatively little attention has been paid to the use of variable charges and subsidies specifically for the purpose of distributional equity in public services. Descriptive studies furnish evidence of the increased take-up of concessionary public transport fares for older people (e.g. Baker and White 2010) and of free leisure opportunities for young people (e.g. Bolton and Martin 2012). Econometric analysis of variable medical prescription charges in Canada suggests that they have the potential to improve distributive efficiency, but that for individuals marginally above subsidy thresholds medical coverage is especially problematic (Alan, Crossley, Grootendorst and Veall 2005). In a similar vein, Doyle's (2007) evaluation of the effects of a reduction in the foster care subsidy in Illinois identifies worse outcomes for vulnerable individuals.

Targeted investments and interventions

Whatever the distributional effects accompanying the tax-and-spend policies of governments, how public expenditure is distributed between different groups may be equally likely to have profound implications for distributive efficiency. For policy-makers and public managers committed to improving distributive efficiency, there are several ways in which efforts to enhance public service output quantity and quality for disadvantaged groups might be made a reality. Generally, such efforts take four main forms: i) distributing grant funding to public services on the basis of the needs of their clientele; ii) making cash or in-kind payments to needy individuals and groups; iii) setting-up bespoke services targeted at disadvantaged or 'hard-to-reach' social groups; and, iv) devoting much greater investment in the standard package of services provided to the geographical areas in which disadvantage is most embedded.

The provision of funding for public services on the basis of some needs-based formula is a commonly accepted principle in the public finance systems of many countries (Boex and Martinez-Vasquez 2005). Typically, needs-based grants are allocated by higher levels of government to lower tiers within the political system or (increasingly, nowadays) are sent direct to service delivery organizations. Although there may be intervening political considerations that shape the final quantum that is allocated by government (Rich 1989), grants distributed on the basis of need are usually based on objective criteria that are intended to be transparent to the casual observer. In general, the size of the clientele being served by a public service is the primary determinant of the grant allocation. Other criteria are likely to include some measure of poverty; population sparsity; different age groups, as relevant; and immigrant population or ethnic heterogeneity. The methodologies used to derive grant allocations are much debated, analysed and reviewed in the public finance literature (e.g. Eyles *et al.* 1991; Darton *et al.* 2010). Much rarer, though, is systematic analysis of whether needs-based grants actually result in improved distributional outcomes. Research that addressed this issue would permit the relative merits of block versus specific grants to be evaluated, as well as whether needs-based funding is more effective than more precisely targeted activities.

Bespoke distributive initiatives range in scale from schemes to address the needs of very specific target groups right through to large-scale urban regeneration projects intended to address place-based disadvantage. The resources for such initiatives can be diverted from within the existing budgets of public services or can be handed down from higher levels of government in the form of specific grants. In both cases, there is an assumption that an increase in public expenditure in the right areas can result in better levels of distributive efficiency across the piece. In general, little attention has been paid to the effectiveness of either type of scheme, let alone whether they are associated with improved distributional equity, or whether any improvements have been achieved within an approved budget constraint.

Interventions targeted at individuals or households in need often involve the use of cash or in-kind transfers to encourage welfare-enhancing choices. Evidence from studies of the use of housing vouchers to encourage poverty deconcentration in US cities offers mixed support for the merits of this form of intervention, with some researchers identifying improved residential mobility (e.g. Kling, Liebman and Katz 2007), and others finding no such improvement (e.g. Jacob 2004). The use of education vouchers for similar reasons may actually have harmed the distributive efficiency of schools provision in the US and Europe (Levin 1998). By contrast, studies of the use of cash transfers in developing countries suggest that they may be an effective means for increasing take-up of education and health services (Rawlings and Rubio 2005). In terms of the distributional effects of in-kind transfers, numerous studies point towards the positive health benefits of the Food Stamp Program in the US (Hoynes, Scanzenbach and Almond 2012), and to the benefits of school-based initiatives for promoting healthy eating (De Sa and Lock 2008).

Another particularly fertile area for research into distributional outcomes has been the introduction of educational policies and practices intended to improve equity in student outcomes. Such initiatives can range from those like *No Child Left Behind* in the US that are developed by central government right the way down to the development of distinctive pedagogical strategies within individual schools. The available evidence from across the globe is, however, somewhat mixed on the merits of such initiatives, with some studies identifying beneficial distributional effects and others not (see Causa and Chapuis 2010, for a review). The health promotion and social work undertaken by many public services is also usually based on the development of strategies for improving outcomes for hard-to-reach groups. Evidence from the US and elsewhere suggests that this work is extremely challenging and resource-intensive, but that improvements in distributional outcomes may result (e.g. Anderson *et al.* 2003; Stevens 2012; Swider 2002).

In addition to policies and practices targeting individual clients or groups of clients, public services are also increasingly involved in large-scale area-based initiatives and anti-poverty strategies intended to address the structural inequalities deeply embedded in disadvantaged communities. The complex array of organizations and agencies involved in these types of activities make the task of managing these initiatives extremely challenging (Sullivan, Barnes and Matka 2006). Related to the managerial problems posed by this organizational complexity are the difficulties surrounding assessments of the impact and effectiveness of area-based initiatives. Nonetheless, the advent of substantial evaluation projects supported by government funding has made it possible for researchers to collect an array of relevant data and to demonstrate that in certain circumstances area-based interventions can have positive out-comes for disadvantaged communities (e.g. Carpenter 2006; Rhodes, Tyler and Brennan 2005).

Professional training, best practices and equality standards

Investments in distributional improvements in the provision of public services are made on the basis of a normative commitment to some principle of dis-tributive justice. Although, it is conceivable that such principles are shared widely throughout society, a growing body of work suggests that public policy-makers and managers have a very distinctive notion of public service that shapes their commitment to initiatives that can assist disadvantaged social groups (Perry 2000). Within developed countries, at least, the management and delivery of public services is therefore often infused with a profound sense of mission, which suggests that *prima facie* the propensity of public servants to contribute more to the community represents a clear improvement in distributive efficiency.

From a managerial perspective, professional training, supportive management practices and the establishment of standards for the fair treatment of citizens are all ways in which distributive efficiency gains from the public service motivation of public officials can potentially be enhanced. Within developed countries, the training of public sector professionals is generally premised on the notion that they behave in an impartial way towards the different client and citizens with whom they have dealings. In this first instance, this applies to the training provided to civil servants and public officials within central state bureau-cracies. In the UK, for example, the civil service has long been bound by structures that encourage the disinterested conduct of public service; something that was formalized in the civil service code of 1996 (Lynn 2006).

The formal training provided to civil servants implies that equality of access and fair treatment are key normative principles underpinning public service at the very highest levels. These principles also apply to the street-level professionals responsible for providing public services. During the period of their professional training, for example, trainee schoolteachers are expected to learn to apply principles of fairness to the ways in which they manage the classroom. Not showing favouritism towards any single student or group of students is an important element of distributing the good of education as equitably as possible. At the same time, teachers are also expected to treat each pupil as an individual with distinctive learning needs, so there is scope for differentiation on the basis of distributional concerns – something that applies to most other professionalized public services. The impact of the professional training of public officials on the equity and efficiency with which public services are delivered is something that simply has not been studied to date, but is clearly something that should be of interest to public service motivation researchers.

Of course, the kinds of professional ideals and practices that can contribute to distributional equity are not just imbibed through the training received by public officials, but can also form an integral part of the human resource management practices within public organizations. Increasingly, the competency-based professional development that has long been available to public officials is being supplemented by bespoke training to improve the ability of professionals to deal with the diverse range of social groups to whom they provide services. Training in customer service excellence, diversity-awareness workshops, equality and diversity champions, women's or minority ethnic support networks and the like, are all commonplace activities within public organizations. For example, the UK Civil Service operates a multitude of different initiatives to support equitable employment and social outcomes (Cabinet Office 2008). In fact, 'diversity management' and equal opportunities policies are now embedded within the personnel management practices of public organizations across the world (Pitts and Wise 2010).

Research on the distributional effects of diversity management in the public sector is largely located within the theories of representative bureaucracy, which assert that public organizations whose employees are more representative of the clientele they serve will do a better job of serving disadvantaged social groups. Recent reviews of the available evidence have found support for this argument, especially at the street-level, where the client–provider interface is closest (Schröter and von Maravic 2012; Walker and Andrews forthcoming). At the same time, there is increasing interest in the effects of the active management of diversity within public organizations on client outcomes and employee outcomes. Several studies suggest that diversity management can have positive benefits for overall levels of employee performance, job satisfaction and turnover (Choi 2009; Pitts 2009). There is also evidence (albeit rather weak) that equality and diversity policies can lead public organizations to become more representative of the population they serve (Groeneveld and Verbeek 2012; Naff and Kellough 2003). However, while all of these studies offer support for the idea that diversity management can improve distributional equity, to date, little is known about the financial costs associated with achieving those improvements.

Linked to the growth of management practices with distinctive distributional effects has been the emergence of audit schemes that assess the standard to which public organizations meet distributional criteria. The rise of certified management excellence initiatives within the public sector (e.g. TQM), has thus been supplemented with bespoke quality standards specifying criteria for equitable public management practices and service outputs. In some cases, these standards are articulated through voluntary schemes that are sponsored by professional bodies or outside agencies, such as the Stonewall Workplace Equality Index, that identifies 'gay-friendly' employers in the UK.

In other cases, equality and diversity quality standards are devised and measured by government itself. For example, in the UK, the Equality Standard for Local Government comprised a points system measuring the distributional effects of management practices within local authorities. In many cases, these schemes are not only a tool for improving distributional outcomes but can be taken as a measure of distributional equity. Precious little attention has been devoted to the impact of equality standards on distributional equity – though, anecdotally, it has been suggested that such schemes were resisted in UK local government on the grounds of cost (Office of the Deputy Prime Minister 2003).

Conclusion

Our reflections on distributive efficiency began with a discussion of the tensions between equity and efficiency that characterize theories of public economics. We emphasized the normative importance of distributive questions, and argued that this inherent normativity implied that principles of distributive justice inevitably underpin decisions about the best way to measure and manage distributive efficiency. Approaches to measuring distributive efficiency were explored by assessing the ways in which public service inputs and outputs could be targeted at certain (usually disadvantaged) social groups, and by reflecting on the costs associated with altering the pattern of distribution of services. Thereafter, the chapter explored three key focal points for initiatives dealing with distributional issues: first, the taxation and expenditure strategies that are implemented at the macro level of public policy; second, the ways in which needs-based grants are allocated and public organizations can be encouraged to target their efforts at specific groups; and, third, the types of professional training, development and standards that can be introduced to shape the attitudes and actions of public officials. At the same time, the relative effectiveness of these alternative approaches to improving distributive efficiency was assessed by taking stock of the scant empirical evidence on their distributional effects. Two principal themes emerged from this discussion of distributive efficiency in the public services.

First, to a greater degree than for the other dimensions of efficiency, the conceptualization, measurement and management of distributive efficiency is a profoundly political process. Quite simply, questions about equality and fairness are contestable to a much greater and more persistent degree than those about output quality, the public sector of the future and citizen satisfaction now. The articulation of an ideal of distributive justice that can secure the support of the citizenry is a challenge for political parties and for policy-makers committed to improving distributional outcomes. This, in turn, places a considerable onus on public managers and organizations to demonstrate that the changes in public service provision made in pursuit of distributive efficiency are having the desired effects.

Second, and relatedly, the alternative approaches to improving distributive efficiency in public services generally imply that some social groups are going to be made worse off in order to improve the lot of other social groups. Although it is possible to raise new revenues to enhance distributive efficiency, in the main, distributional improvements are achieved by redirecting existing resources to areas of designated need. This again makes the public justification of policy and its management on this dimension of efficiency utterly essential. Unfortunately, the sparse evidence base on the impact of policies to promote distributive efficiency offers only limited support for some of the most common approaches used to deliver equity improvements within budgetary limits.

The reflections on distributive efficiency developed in this chapter have drawn upon the ideas about the measurement and management of productive efficiency that we advanced in the previous chapter. Still, we have also emphasized that the distributive dimension of the efficiency captures important features of the management and provision of public services that are distinctive and that speak to the rationale behind state provision of public goods and the notion of public service itself. In fact, distributive efficiency, in particular, encapsulates the inherently normative nature of democratic public administration. Distributional concerns do not only give voice to the idea of a public purpose, but also the kind of public philosophy that underpins that purpose – something that can also be said for its justice-orientated counterpart – dynamic efficiency – to which we now turn.

5   Dynamic efficiency

The two dimensions of efficiency considered so far are both static in that they focus on the management of a given set of resources at a particular point of time. By contrast, the concept of dynamic efficiency, as economists express it, considers the management of resources over time: between current and future consumption. A dynamically efficient position is attained when enough is invested today to maintain or increase our productive capacity tomorrow, but not investing to the point where there will be underused capital and an unnecessary restriction of current consumption (Stavins, Wagner and Wagner 2003). Failures of dynamic efficiency have implications for productive capacity over time but also for equity between current and future generations.

The equity effect results from one generation carrying too heavy, or too light, a burden relative to another. If there has been an over-accumulation of capital, as Abel *et al.* (1989: 1) explain: 'A Pareto improvement can be achieved … by allowing the current generation to devour a portion of the capital stock and then holding constant the consumption of all future generations.' By contrast, excessive consumption today – and the correlative borrowing and resource depletion which might be associated with it – will shift a cost, or burden, to younger or future generations. A popular version of this scenario is described by Willetts (2011) in *The Pinch*. The Baby Boom generation (1945–65) have, according to Willetts, benefited from an unparalleled accumulation of wealth at the expense of subsequent generations. The welfare state, the housing market and arrangements for occupational pensions, have all worked to the advantage of the post-war generation at the expense of their children, who, claims Willetts (2011), are finding it correspondingly more difficult to buy their own house, start a family and save for their own retirement. While we may agree that neither earlier nor later generations are likely, in the much cited but disputed words of Harold Macmillan to 'have it so good', it is not clear what the balance between generations should be.

As Stavins *et al.* (2003: 341) explain, however, the strict Pareto criterion 'is virtually never taken as a guide for public policy' suggesting in its place a Kaldor–Hicks (Hicks 1939) type analysis in which 'the world is viewed as being made better off if the magnitude of gains and the magnitude of losses are such that the gainers can fully compensate the losers for their losses and still be better off themselves.' Barrell and Weale (2010) consider three notions of intergenerational equity: that each cohort pays its own way; that resources are reallocated between generations to achieve an optimum position over time; or that resources are reallocated so that generations alive at the same time have similar living standards. Although theoretically interesting, the issue of intergenerational equity does not loom large in debates about public borrowing and expenditure. Whether because the comparison between what are in many ways incommensurable generations is too difficult to grasp, or because human lives are sufficiently long and indeterminate to give all of us a stake in the future, it is the question of whether we are making the right investment decisions today, to maintain or increase our productive capacity tomorrow, which predominates in debates about current versus future consumption.

Future productive capacity is in part determined by the stock of physical capital – buildings, machinery, IT – which needs to be procured and maintained. But increasing future capacity is not just about investment in physical capital. In the same way that a new road or railway provides a flow of future benefits, so too might investment in human, social, knowledge and natural capital. As Adler and Kwon (2002: 21) explain, with specific reference to social capital, these are long-lived assets 'into which other resources can be invested, with the expectation of a future (albeit uncertain) flow of benefits'. Although there are no internationally agreed conventions for the definition and measurement of investment in these other forms of capital, human capital may be built through current spending on education and healthcare; knowledge capital (Grossman and Helpman 1990), by spending on research and development; and social capital through expenditure on a series of community or network development-type activities. Natural capital presents perhaps the greatest challenges of definition and measurement, but it may at least be protected by appropriate expenditures on resource management programmes. In its broadest sense then, the notion of dynamic efficiency addresses the balances between all of these stocks and flows over time.

While economists differ in their assessment of dynamic efficiency (Abel *et al.* 1989), they are agreed that freely determined market interest rates should at least, in theory, ensure an efficient balance between current and future consumption (Barrell and Weale 2010). In a free market, investors will put resources into future productive capacity so long as it is profitable for them to do so. The over-accumulation of capital – and a corresponding decline in the return on these assets – is clearly a situation investors would try to avoid. There are however, as Partha and David (1994: 487) explain, 'no economic forces that operate automatically to maintain dynamic efficiency' in the public realm. Politicians and public managers make decisions to build schools, hospitals and transport infrastructure without the prospect of a cashable return on their investment. With few straightforward ways of valuing the return to capital – and very short time horizons dictated by their term of office – politicians may underinvest in desirable projects but overinvest in vanity projects.

In the absence of automatic processes which operate in the private realm, public managers need ways of measuring and managing dynamic efficiency so that they can make good decisions about investment in capital projects and prioritize between different types of current expenditure. Accordingly, as in previous chapters, we begin by considering problems of measurement before reviewing the policies pursued by governments to ensure dynamic efficiency.

Concepts and indicators

Like the other dimensions of efficiency we have considered, dynamic efficiency can be seen as an input–output ratio, but in this case the inputs occur at an earlier point in time than the outputs. Almost any relevant indicator of performance can be used as the output or outcome in the dynamic efficiency equation. The performance of the economy may, for example, be measured by economic growth over a sustained period. Smaller units of government may be more interested in area growth measurements, of one form or another, while individual agencies may look at specific outputs or outcomes whether in terms, for example, of education, healthcare or transport.

The investment side of the equation is more difficult. Endogenous growth theories suggest that the productive capacity of an economy can be increased by investments in human and physical capital (Barro 1991). While expenditures on physical capital – schools, hospitals and so forth – are easily defined and publicly reported, some of the other dimensions of capital present more of a challenge. Increasingly, however, there are a series of accepted approaches to investment in human, knowledge and even social capital. Investment in natural capital is more difficult still, but again a number of resource management strategies have been developed, even if there is not a consensus on which represents the best type of investment. While much of the intellectual effort to establish indicators is focused on the national or country level, the same principles can be applied to specific organizations. Indeed there is more evidence to support the efficacy of investment in social capital for organizations than there is for countries or regions (Westlund and Adam 2011).

Measuring inputs and outputs over time provides only a lagging indicator of dynamic efficiency. This approach tells us about the efficiency of resource decisions taken in the past but not about the efficiency implications of decisions taken today. But public managers, and their political masters, want to know whether they are making the right resource decisions to improve performance in the future. To address this problem, governments sometimes use leading indicators of dynamic efficiency which are focused on the patterns of performance, the kinds of decisions, or the organizational characteristics, that researchers think will lead to dynamic efficiency. The next section reviews three types of measure – outputs, inputs and leading indicators – used to gauge dynamic efficiency before we go on to consider the kinds of policies intended to improve dynamic efficiency in the final section.

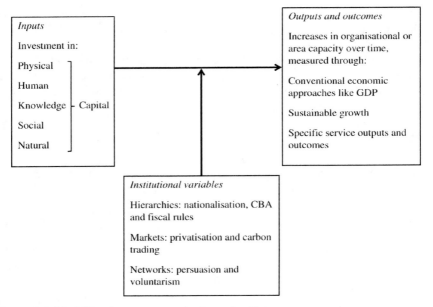

Figure 5.1 Modelling improvements in dynamic efficiency.

Outputs and outcomes

Dynamic efficiency requires the management of resources over time in such a way as to 'continually "shift" the production possibilities curve to the right' (De Soto 2009: 8). Measures of Gross Domestic Product (GDP) provide perhaps the best established indication of the increasing capacity of a country or region. Economic growth – as indicated by sustained increases in GDP over a sustained period of time – is testament to increased economic activity but also to the improvements in welfare associated with it. There are debates about how GDP figures need to be adjusted for imports and exports, inflation, exchange rates, capital depreciation, government intervention and so forth, and questions too, about the time period necessary to distinguish short-term fluctuations from long-term growth (Nordhaus and Tobin 1972; Landefeld, Seskin and Fraumeni 2008). More profoundly, however, some economists question whether traditional national income figures capture sustainable growth and whether adjustments need to be made for the depletion of non-renewable resources and environmental damage (Heal 2012). Some measures of sustainable development or sustainable growth may then prove a more appropriate measure of progress over time than national income (Wilson, Tyedmers and Pelot 2007). Others, however, question the merit of any of these national accounting exercises, and the implicit commitment to continual growth which goes with them, suggesting instead that subjective measures of happiness or wellbeing may prove a more appropriate indication of progress over time. As Layard (2006: 24) puts it: 'despite massive increases in purchasing power, people in the West are no happier than they were fifty years ago'.

While regional governments may use income data to measure their performance, these broad measures of economic activity are unlikely to be appropriate for lower levels of government or indeed for agencies tasked with the delivery of particular services. Police, transport, health or education providers will wish to see improvements in specific output or outcome measures of their performance over time. In such a way, school managers may be focused on improving levels of literacy and numeracy of their graduating students, measured perhaps through successful test or examination results. Hospitals will wish to see improvement in the success rates of different treatment options, and a decline in the infection or mortality rates. Transport authorities may have a view to easing congestion or switching journeys to more sustainable modes of transportation. Police authorities may be interested in arrest rates, reported crime or perceptions of community safety. Whatever measures are used, they need to be reliable over a decent period of time since short-term fluctuations are unlikely to be related to long-term changes in the performance of a region or organization.

Inputs

The first and most obvious candidate input to any analysis of dynamic efficiency is, of course, investment in physical capital. Inputs of this type have the advantage that they are easily measured since most government and public agencies report capital investment in one form or another. In such a way, investments in physical capital can be treated as inputs likely to be associated, at some later point, with improved performance. Studies of economic growth provide some support for this contention (Barro 1991). Aschauer (1989: 20) finds 'strong support for the idea that public investment is a critical determinant of labor productivity growth'. Mittnik and Neumann's (2001: 445) analysis of six industrial countries also 'suggests that public investment tends to exert positive influence on GDP'. Studies of particular services – like school education – also suggest that investments in physical capital can pay a performance dividend (Crampton 2009).

Investment in human capital has long been associated with improved economic performance (Barro 1991). There is disagreement, however, about the most appropriate way of measuring the investment. Commentators largely dismiss the efficacy of simple increases in resources invested in education and training (Hanushek 1989; 1997), suggesting instead that investments in education need to be directed at securing specific changes in the way in which education services are provided (Woesmann, 2007; OECD 2010). It may, therefore, be more appropriate to measure the investment in specific interventions targeted perhaps at increased enrolment rates (Barro 1991), time spent in education (Barro and Lee 2010) or education quality (Barro 2001).

While measures of human capital capture the investment in people, other forms of knowledge lie outside human minds. The concept of knowledge capital tries to capture the institutional arrangements which hold or communicate knowledge. Furmana *et al.* (2002: 903) describe a 'national innovative capacity' which reflects both the high 'quality human resources' but also a series of other variables from 'an ample supply of risk capital' to basic research infrastructure in universities. Increases in the financial resources for research and development and investments in the research capacity of universities may then be regarded as inputs likely to sustain or increase knowledge capital.

Social capital 'consists' according to Westlund and Adam (2010: 897) 'of networks of actors' and the norms and values that hold them together. There is increasing, although not unequivocal, evidence that social capital can bestow a series of economic benefits. Westlund and Adam (2010: 897) explain that: 'Trust reduces transaction costs' by limiting the need 'for detailed contracts, controls and surveillance'. But it also 'speeds up informal information flows and knowledge exchange' fostering the development and adoption of innovations (Westlund and Adam 2010: 897). Supporting the hypothesis, Knack and Keefer (1997: 1252) find that levels of 'trust and civic cooperation' are indeed associated 'with stronger economic performance'. Casey (2004) too, finds a strong correlation between membership of civic associations and trade unions and economic performance. While investments in social capital are difficult to specify, commentators focus first on attempts to provide the right kind of institutional context – in terms of the regulation of social and economic conduct – and second on the broadening and deepening of civic and economic networks.

Finally, the recognition that many of the resources underpinning current levels of consumption are finite and non-renewable suggests that governments also need to have regard to the management of natural capital (Pearce and Atkinson 1993; Arrow *et al.* 1995; Heal 2012). The natural environment can be treated as a dimension of capital to the extent that it provides, in Daly's (1994) words 'source' and 'sink' capacity. Source capacity is provided by the stock of 'natural resources or environmental assets, such as oceans, forests or agricultural land, that yields a flow of useful goods and services now and into the future' (MacDonald 1999: 74). Sink capacity is provided by the assimilative capacity for waste. The two services provided by natural capital suggest two reasons for managing it. As a source, natural resources are either non-renewable – in the case of oil, copper or uranium – or fragile (fish or timber) in that they need to be harvested sustainably. As a sink, we need to ensure that our wastes do not overpower the natural environment's assimilative capacity. Failure to manage natural capital as a source would, in simple terms, mean that we run out of natural resources; failure to manage it as a sink would eventually mean that we start to poison ourselves. Either way, the state of natural capital presents 'limits to growth' (England 2000) and good reason to manage it sustainably.

But if the natural environment is a form of capital, it is not clear how governments can invest in it. Aside from the case of so-called 'cultivated natural capital' like fish farms, vineyards or orchards (Brand 2009: 606), we cannot invest in natural capital in the traditional sense. Rather, as Daly (1994) explains, investment in renewable natural resources means limiting the harvest or maintaining it at a level compatible with its growth or replacement. For non-renewable forms of natural capital, 'the question' as Daly puts it 'is not to invest but how best to liquidate the inventory, and what to do with the net wealth realised from the liquidation' (Daly 1994: 32). Investment in natural capital might then mean a number of different things. Investment in physical capital like windmills, or solar energy would allow a switch from non-renewable to renewable energy. Investment in a fishery protection pro- gramme may halt the depletion of a stock in such a way as to make continuing harvests sustainable. Or investment may simply mean consumption delayed – in the form of deliberately unexploited resources, or invested revenues in sovereign wealth funds – with a view to making a limited resource last longer into the future.

Leading indicators

The inputs and outputs described above need to be collected over a sustained period to avoid mistaking short-term variations for long-term changes in capacity. The disadvantage of this, however, is that measurements over time provide only a lagging indication of dynamic efficiency. They tell us about the efficiency of resource decisions taken in the past but not about the efficiency of decisions taken today. To solve this problem, governments sometimes use leading indicators of dynamic efficiency, which are focused on patterns of performance or organizational characteristics believed to be associated with dynamic efficiency.

Research in this area is perhaps most advanced in the area of growth theory. Based on analysis of growth rates across countries and over time, economists point to a series of institutional arrangements which are taken to be precursors of economic growth. The World Economic Forum uses measures of this kind – 12 pillars of competitiveness as they describe them, embracing amongst other things public institutions, education, labour markets and innovation – to construct a league table of the 'foundations of national com- petitiveness' (Schwab 2012: 4). The league table, and the measures at its heart, are useful in that they give an early warning of future performance and point to the kinds of reforms governments might want to make to improve their competitiveness and growth.

UK regulators have long used a similar approach to judge the prospects for improvement of individual public agencies. In the same way that the World Economic Forum identifies its 12 pillars of competitiveness, UK regulators point to a series of organizational characteristics which they believe provide an indication of the prospects of improvement of an individual agency. The local government Comprehensive Performance Assessment scheme, for example assessed individual councils' 'ability to improve' by considering amongst other things their prioritization, performance measurement, investment and learning (Andrews *et al.* 2005: 642). School inspectors try to assess whether 'leaders, managers and governors are judged to be capable of securing improvement' by reference to vision, expectations, professional development, parental engagement and so forth (OFSTED 2013: 16–20). While the ambition of these schemes is laudable, the difficulty is that the evidence base linking these organizational characteristics with performance and improvement is limited to say the very least. So, while an individual council or school may display the *right* characteristics at the time of inspection, it may then fail to deliver the expected improvement at a later point in time.

Policies

In general, it is reasonable to assume that governments try to make dynamically efficient public spending decisions, although as we explained in chapter two, the rules of the political market do not always reward dynamic efficiency in the way we would like. But aside from striving to include dynamic considerations in their decision-making about current and future consumption, governments have developed a number of policies, devices or practices which are intended to improve dynamic efficiency. We consider these under the headings of the main inputs we have already introduced.

Physical capital

On the face of it, investment in the stock of physical capital should present fewest difficulties. There is little controversy about how to make those investments (as there is with our four other types of capital). Conventions for the measurement and reporting of investment in physical capital are well established and there is good evidence that these investments increase productive capacity. The difficulty, such as it is, lies in the tendency for politicians to borrow for current consumption rather than capital investment; to underinvest in physical capital assets; and on occasion, to overinvest in vanity projects – like Tony Blair's infamous Millennium Dome – which may play well with voters in the short term but which are economically questionable in the long term.

As we suggested in chapter two, all three are understandable if not inevitable consequences of democratic systems which elect politicians for relatively short terms of office. With short political careers, elected politicians have few incentives to make budget decisions today which will bear fruit long after they have left office. Policy in this area is then based on the three goals of limiting borrowing for current consumption, increasing investment in appropriate physical assets but avoiding investment in vanity projects. Governments have put in place a number of initiatives intended to achieve these goals. We consider three below: cost–benefit analysis, privatization and the adoption of fiscal rules.

Perhaps the oldest device intended to ensure that future benefits are factored into current decision-making is cost–benefit analysis (CBA). Prest and Turvey

(1965) track its origins back to 1844. By valuing the wider costs and benefits of a particular project (which may be a physical investment like a new road or even a new treatment option in medicine) and then discounting in some way for the passage of time, CBA promises a rigorous method for project appraisal. But even when interpreted in relatively narrow terms, CBA presents formidable challenges. Vickerman (2007: 608) concludes that 'generally the longer the planning period, the larger the investment, and the more complex is the project, the larger is the likelihood of significant errors in the original forecasts.' Indeed, Mackie and Preston (1998) identify twenty-one sources of error and bias – from unclear objectives to undue optimism – in transport appraisals. Prest and Turvey (1965: 730–31) argue, however, that CBA does at least force 'those responsible to quantify costs and benefits as far as possible rather than rest content with vague qualitative judgments or personal hunches'. In such a way it 'can help in the rejection of inferior projects, which are nevertheless promoted for empire-building or pork-barrel reasons' (Prest and Turvey 1965: 730–31).

But does it work? Evidence on the effectiveness of CBA in guiding investment decisions is mixed. Eliasson and Lundberg's (2012) review of the transport literature suggests a 'weak or non-existent' 'connection between CBA results and investment decisions'. Their analysis of 'the Swedish National Transport Investment Plan 2010–21' however provides 'a fairly strong (although obviously far from perfect) correlation between CBA results and investment decisions' (Eliasson and Lundberg 2012). Annema *et al.* (2007: 146) consider the effects of the adoption of standardized CBA procedures for new infrastructure projects in the Netherlands, finding that it has 'actually supported and improved the quality of decision-making' but 'it is not known what would have happened if decision-making in these cases had been supported in the pre-CBA fashion.'

CBA is difficult precisely because it requires analysts to put monetary figures on things – like journey times, amenity and species diversity – which are not normally valorized. Instead of guessing what those values might be, a more durable solution may be provided by the partial or complete privatization of the services or assets in question. By clearly demarcating property rights and monetizing the benefits flowing from capital assets, privatization may lead to improved investment decisions and gains in dynamic efficiency. Alexandre and Charreaux (2004) consider exactly this possibility in their study of French privatization. While they find some evidence of increased investment, many of their results are not statistically significant or are rooted in decisions taken prior to privatization. Similarly, Cabeza García and Gómez Ansón (2007: 390) find 'significant improvements in firms' long-term industry-adjusted profitability and efficiency' but after correcting for industry effects they 'cannot confirm an increase in investment' (Cabeza García and Gómez Ansón 2007: 407). Arocena and Oliveros (2012: 464) do, however, find that the efficiency (when capital assets are treated as an input) of twenty formerly state-owned enterprises did 'significantly increase after their privatization' suggesting perhaps a tendency of state-owned enterprises to over rather than underinvest.

The same theory informed the development of the UK government's Private Finance Initiative (PFI) (Clark *et al.* (2002)). By privatizing public infrastructure investment, the PFI monetized the flow of benefits from physical capital and therefore attracted private sector investors into a variety of capital projects from bridges and motorways to hospitals and schools. Turning public infrastructure into private investments had the additional benefit of removing the expenditure from public balance sheets, thus allowing politicians to have both high levels of current spending *and* infrastructure renewal. There seems little doubt that PFI allowed an increase in investment beyond that which would have been achieved without it. That is not to say, however, that all of those investments are dynamically efficient (Shaoul, Stafford and Stappleton 2011). Critics argue that the same investments could have been funded much more cheaply through the public sector and that while the private backers may have secured a good return on their stake, the broader costs remain firmly in the public realm (Gaffney *et al.* 1999).

Our third mechanism – fiscal or budget rules – are intended to provide an institutional check on spending and borrowing decisions. Schaechter *et al.* (2012) report a rapid expansion in the adoption of fiscal rules across the world from 5 countries in 1980 to 76 by 2012. Almost all US states have balanced budget rules which forbid borrowing for current consumption (Bohn and Inman 1996: 13–76). In the UK, the erstwhile Chancellor of the Exchequer, Gordon Brown, promised that the Labour government would abide by the 'golden rule' borrowing only to invest and 'not to fund current expenditure' (Sawyer 2007: 887). The architects of the policy argued that by focusing on the public sector borrowing requirement, previous governments had been guilty of 'a considerable under-investment in public assets' (cited in Sawyer 2007: 888). By following the golden rule, the then Labour government promised to improve both the UK's economic performance and intergenerational fairness.

At the supranational level, the EU's Stability and Growth Pact sought to limit member states to a budget deficit of 3% of GDP, and accumulated debt of 60% of GDP. The financial crisis of 2008 and the developing Eurozone crisis which followed made it 'clear to all' as Frankel and Schreger (2013: 248), put it 'that the Stability and Growth Pact (SGP) has failed to keep budget deficits and debt levels of Eurozone members within the limits specified'. They attribute its failings to the tendency of countries 'in danger of breaching the limit' to produce 'over-optimistic forecasts' which gave the appearance of compliance at least with the spirit of the pact (Frankel and Schreger 2013: 271). Frankel and Schreger (2013: 271) conclude that 'national budget balance rules or independent fiscal institutions that provide their own independent forecasts help to reduce this bias.'

With the exception of the EU's stability growth pact (Schuknecht *et al.* 2011), most of the analysis of fiscal or budget rules suggests, as Bohn and Inman (1996:

63) put it, that 'balanced-budget rules, appropriately constructed and enforced, reduce the propensity of states to run deficits'. Indeed, the problem may be that they work too well. Excessively tight rules run the risk of restricting desirable investments in capital projects. The solution as Gramlich (1994: 1194) suggests, is to 'change policies to permit states to go on their own on infrastructure investment, cutting states loose from the federal grant system and giving states their own source of revenue and power to make key decisions.' In exactly this way the UK government blamed 'a highly centralised system' governing local government borrowing and investment for 'very low levels of conventional capital spending by authorities' (Hood *et al.* 2007: 58). In a bid to address this problem the rules were relaxed in 2003 under the prudential borrowing arrangements which allow local governments to make their own decisions about capital expenditure against the backdrop of a prudential code based, in essence, on a number of measures of affordability (Bailey *et al.* 2010).

Whatever rules are adopted there is, inevitably, a danger that they will at some point fail to suit changing economic circumstances. The counter cyclical expenditures of almost all governments since 2008 have made a mockery of what seemed like perfectly sensible rules adopted in the preceding decade. The difficulty of designing effective but durable rules is made more acute by the fact that many of the investments we have described – and go on to consider below – are not traditionally categorized as capital investment.

Human capital

Although the idea of human capital – and the associated suggestion that investments can be made in it – has been around for a long time, unlike physical capital, there are no established conventions for defining and measuring those investments. Schultz (1961: 1) describes direct investments in 'education, health and internal migration' as clear cases of investments in human capital, but he also includes on-the-job training and the earnings and leisure time 'forgone by mature students'.

Starting with health, it is clearly the case that humans require some minimal level of investment to keep them alive and healthy. As Bloom *et al.* (2004: 1) put it: 'Healthier workers are physically and mentally more energetic and robust. They are more productive and earn higher wages. They are also less likely to be absent from work because of illness.' Based on data from a panel of countries observed over a thirty-year period, Bloom *et al.* (2004: 11) find that 'health has a positive and statistically significant effect on economic growth. It suggests that a one-year improvement in a population's life expectancy contributes to an increase of 4% in output.' Investments which improve life expectancy are then good for future growth. Within the category of health expenditure, health economists point to the relative efficiency of expenditure on health promotion over acute care (Fries *et al.* 1993).

Aside from investments in health, human capital needs to be developed through education and training. Here, however, the evidence becomes more mixed. Simple financial measures of spending on education are unlikely to capture the kind of inputs that are needed. Researchers disagree about the categories of educational expenditure which really count in the business of improving future capacity. Hanushek and Woessmann (2011: 444) ask, provocatively, should governments 'focus on decent basic skills for the whole population or on nurturing top scientists and engineers?'

Based on an analysis of PISA test scores and long-term economic performance, Hanushek and Woessmann (2011: 444) argue 'that direct measures of educational outcomes, in terms of cognitive skills on international achievement tests, emerge as the one strong policy factor underlying growth differences across OECD countries'. Tertiary attainment, by contrast, 'is not significantly associated with long-run growth differences across OECD countries' (Hanushek and Woessmann 2011: 478). Knudsen *et al.* (2006: 10161) too argue persuasively that 'the most cost-effective strategy for strengthening the future American workforce is to invest greater human and financial resources in the social and cognitive environments of children who are disadvantaged'. A prescription which sits comfortably with the suggestion from criminologists that early intervention to combat the known causes of delinquency and criminality can represent better value for money than future spending on policing and prisons (Farrington and Welsh 2008).

Even if we accept that politicians should focus on basic skills rather than the higher-level education provided by universities, it is not at all clear what sorts of investments governments should make to improve basic skills teaching. Hanushek and Woessmann (2011: 479) point to 'evidence from both within and across countries' of a 'positive impact of competition among schools, of accountability and student testing, and of local school autonomy in decision making'. Whether reforms of this sort require increased spending on education takes us back to arguments considered in chapter three.

Knowledge capital

Aside from the investment in human capital, the development of knowledge requires investment in broader processes of research, development and dissemination. Dasgupta and David (1994: 489) explain, however, that a 'systematic market failure' – rooted in uncertainty and the difficulty of protecting intellectual property – 'results in societal under-investment in science'. In such a way, a case can be made, as Dodgson *et al.* (2011: 1146) put it, for public investment in basic research, patent protection and venture capital.

Rodriguez-Pose and Crescenzi (2008: 54) describe a linear model where the 'higher the investment in R&D, the higher the innovative capacity, and the higher the economic growth'. Empirical research bears this out. Salter and Martin (2001: 513–14) report that 'studies show a large, positive contribution of academic research to economic growth' and that specific studies of publicly funded research projects point to 'a large positive pay off'. While the correlations are not disputed, the mechanisms are. Bilbao-Osorio and Rodriguez-Pose (2004: 452) find that the 'impact of R&D investment on innovation' although positive 'is contingent on the socio-economic structure of the region'. Rodriguez-Pose and Crescenzi (2008: 64) describe a 'social filter' – measured in terms of the level of higher education, employment in agriculture and the age of the population – which determines the capacity to 'assimilate whatever research is being generated locally or in neighbouring regions and to transform it into innovation and economic activity'. Salter and Martin (2001: 528) conclude, however, that 'it is difficult to arrive at simple policy prescriptions' because the 'benefits are often subtle, heterogeneous, difficult to track or measure, and mostly indirect'.

Focused on this broad issue, commentators increasingly describe national or regional innovation systems made up of a variety of organizations – including firms, universities, technology-transfer agencies, consultants, skills-development organizations, funding bodies and firms – with linkages as Cooke *et al.* (1997: 478) put it 'specified in terms of flows of knowledge and information, flows of investment funding, flows of authority and even more informal arrangements such as networks, clubs, fora and partnerships'. As Dodgson *et al.* (2011: 1146) explain: 'Successful economies are those which have robust, but adaptable, network connections that enable organizations to translate new knowledge into viable innovations and enhanced productive capacity.' Lundvall (2007: 101) observes, however, that each national system develops its own 'unique dynamics' reflecting 'an intricate interplay between micro and macro phenomena'. Policies to improve the working of these systems are hard to specify.

Social capital

If investments in knowledge capital are hard to specify, social capital is even more problematic. Indeed, some commentators suggest that its deep historical roots mean that it 'should be treated as an exogenously given endowment' (Adler and Kwon 2002: 21) and, that by implication, it is unlikely to respond to investment. Others argue, as Woolcock (1998: 157) puts it, that a society's stock of social capital will be 'enhanced by dismantling the state'; a prescription that sits comfortably with the British Government's Big Society programme. An attempt, as Kisby describes it, to empower communities and promote volunteering which has been introduced alongside marked reductions in public expenditure (Kisby 2010).

Many commentators though – including Adler and Kwon (2002: 21) – maintain that 'at least under some circumstances', social capital is 'constructible through deliberate actions'. Lorenzen (2007: 813) maintains that 'public authorities' have a 'vital role in setting this process in motion'. Indeed he recommends 'inspiring and forcing regions with a low stock of social capital to invest in it' (Lorenzen 2007: 813). Three different approaches to the development of social capital are apparent in the literature (Woolcock and Narayan

2000). The first – the bonding strategy – emphasizes the importance of close relations or 'strong ties' between members of an organization or community. On this basis, Lorenzen (2007: 812) recommends government support for civic associations related to 'leisure, culture and various unions' with a view to maintaining 'social stability and institutional learning'. At the intra-organizational level, Adler and Kwon (2002: 35) point to the need to nurture motivation but also to provide resources in the form of 'collaborative technologies, such as shared knowledge repositories, chat rooms, and videoconferences'.

The bridging strategy, by contrast, prioritizes the 'weak ties' associated with broader exposure to new and different sources of information. In this vein Lorenzen (2007: 812) suggests that efforts to open 'a region to outside influences, competences and people' will ease the transfer of knowledge across boundaries. Governments can also use procurement processes to 'loosen' or 'demonopolise' (Lorenzen 2007: 812) markets, facilitating 'institutional unlearning' where necessary and then redesigning 'social conventions into co-operation'. He gives the example of public–private partnerships and prestige projects as sparking 'a new regional game' based on cooperation rather than competition (Lorenzen 2007: 812–13).

Finally, the institutional strategy points to the role of governments in establishing an environment that is conducive to the development of social capital. At the very least, this requires 'formal institutional rules that constrain the government from acting arbitrarily' (Knack and Keefer 1997: 1284). Even sceptics like Fukuyama (2001: 18) acknowledge that 'Educational institutions', for example, 'do not simply transmit human capital, they also pass on social capital in the form of social rules and norms'. More ambitiously, Wilson (1997: 754) argues that the challenge of building social capital calls for a re-skilling of public managers in terms of their ability to work with citizens and communities in such a way as to 'create the kind of "public space" that generates social capital'. More specifically, Warner (2001: 189) explains that: 'To effectively build social capital, local government must share autonomy with citizens' by 'decentralizing programs to the neighborhood level' with a view to 'shifting its emphasis from controller, regulator and provider to new roles as catalyst, convener and facilitator'. 'Where these formal governmental institutions can be decentralized and control shared with local residents', Warner (2001: 189) claims, 'the impact on social capital development and governmental transformation can be dramatic.'

Natural capital

If we assume that there are limits to the substitutability of capital goods – so that the depletion of natural resources cannot be fully compensated for by technological developments – then a pattern of current consumption which is heavily dependent on, or damaging of, non-renewable resources will damage future productive capacity. For those who accept the logic of this argument

(Victor 1991), an investment in the sustainable management of natural capital will yield a flow of future benefits.

As we have already suggested, some investments in natural capital are easily conceived. Physical investments in windmills, or solar power, allow a switch from non-renewable to renewable energy. Many other investments – like those intended to ensure sustainable harvests for example – are, however, harder to classify and even more difficult to deliver. But what sorts of policy intervention are likely to foster these types of investment? In their reconsideration of Hardin's *Tragedy of the Commons*, Ostrom *et al.* (1999) suggest that there are three approaches: nationalization, privatization or mutualization. All three are apparent in the sustainability strategies developed across the world.

The nationalization strategy has been deployed as part of the EU's common fishery policy. In a bid to manage its cod stocks, the EU imposed total allowable catches alongside a number of other regulations. Kraak *et al.* (2013: 210) report, however, a 'failure to adequately implement the plan and achieve its objectives.' They attribute this failure to the fact that 'fisher behaviour was not fully taken into account in the design, the impact assessment, and the annual implementation of the plan' (Kraak *et al.* 2013: 210). They suggest that more participatory arrangements – in which local fishing communities play a part in designing a fish management policy – may prove more effective.

Although there are few examples of the wholesale privatization of the commons envisaged by Hardin, governments have used market-based instruments to address the problem of missing markets which he alluded to. The clearest examples are seen in the emission trading programmes developed in the US and EU. Schemes of this type still rely on hierarchical authority to establish the rules of the market, but they deliver change through market incentives unleashed by the trading of permits rather than hierarchical coercion (Baldwin 2008). In theory at least, the investment in natural capital is made by private sector industries incentivized to reduce their pollution. Based on a sample of five German generation companies, Hoffmann (2007: 472) finds some evidence of increased investment in low-risk, short-life, low-carbon projects, but 'large-scale investment decisions with long amortization times' are not, he concludes, currently driven by the trading scheme. On the basis of a wider review of the literature Zhang and Wei (2010: 1810) conclude that 'existing research results do not support the significant economic effect' of the EU emission trading scheme on 'energy technology investment'.

Finally, the third approach suggested by Ostrom, relies on the voluntary actions of individuals galvanized by common values and trust. This approach is at the heart of the UK government's attempt to increase household waste minimization and recycling. Unlike some other countries, the UK has decided not to incentivize recycling through market-based instruments, or through coercive regulations (Bulkeley and Gregson 2009). Rather, UK governments have chosen to invest in recycling facilities and education campaigns on the presumption that householders who think green will act green and recycle. Based on an analysis of recycling in Minnesota, Sidique *et al.* (2010) find support for incentivization and coercion strategies, but they also find that: 'Educating the public on recycling' as measured over a three-year period also increases the recycling rate such that: 'Spending one dollar per person per year will increase the rate of recycling by approximately 2%.'

Conclusion

The management of dynamic efficiency presents formidable challenges to politicians and managers. First, it requires them to forgo consumption today in return for the promise of improved performance tomorrow. Second, the imperfect substitutability of different forms of capital requires a decision about which type of investment promises the best value for money. Should a unit of tax revenue, earmarked for investment, be spent on physical, human, knowledge, social or natural capital? Third, dynamic efficiency requires politicians and managers to make those decisions in the face of unavoidable uncertainty. In the absence of the clear signals – in terms of a cashable return on investment provided by correctly working free markets – we cannot be sure, even years later, whether the investments we made were the right ones. Indeed, as we saw in chapter two, there are some reasons to think that the political market – such as it is – might send precisely the wrong signals about future decision-making to politicians and managers. Fourth, although academics recognize the different capitals we have discussed, conventional standards of accounting and reporting do not. Investments in human, knowledge, social and natural capital must, as a result, compete against other often more pressing demands of current consumption.

Finally, as well as considering the relative merits of different types of investment, public managers also need to consider possible interactions between them. There is evidence that some investments work well together. Perhaps most clearly, human capital in the form of a highly educated and skilled work force complements investments in knowledge capital (Salter and Martin 2001). An educated workforce forms part of the 'social filter' which determines the effectiveness of investments in research and development (Rodriguez-Pose and Crescenzi 2008). Not all investments however, are so compatible. New fossil-fuel burning power stations may promise a flow of future benefits, in the form of cheap and dependable energy, but they are clearly at odds with the need to protect our natural capital.

The policies we have considered – from technical fixes like cost–benefit analysis and sustainability indicators to ambitious policy interventions like privatization on the one hand and nationalization on the other – are intended to improve the dynamic efficiency of capital investment decisions. Evidence of their effectiveness is, as we have seen, sometimes equivocal. Other fixes – like generational accounts (Auerbach, Gokhale and Kotlikoff 1994) and no doubt many other policies we have not managed to include – may, if adopted, prove more successful. It seems unlikely, however, that there could be an omnibus answer to the challenge of managing dynamic efficiency. That is to say the business of juggling the relative priorities of current and future consumption seems likely to remain essentially political if not essentially contested.

6   Allocative efficiency

Allocative efficiency addresses the question of whether resources are allocated to their most productive and satisfying uses. Are the goods and services produced in the economy ones that are valued by citizens? Economic theory suggests that allocative efficiency will be ensured by the interaction of supply and demand. The countervailing forces – of excess supply driving prices down and scarcity pushing them up – should deliver a market clearing price and an economically efficient allocation of resources without the need for central planning or intervention.

In public management, the services provided by the state – from defence, health care and education to street lighting and open spaces – are sometimes collectively consumed, often free at the point of use and almost always funded by taxation. In this context, allocative efficiency is concerned with the extent to which governments deliver value for money in terms of the balance between the services provided and the level of tax collected (Oates 1969). In such a way, the allocative dimension provides an overarching account of the three dimensions we have already considered. Governments collect tax revenues and then spend them on service production, redistributive activities of one form or another and investments in capital with a view to increasing welfare. An allocatively efficient position is attained when it is impossible to improve satisfaction by changing the make-up of this tax-service package.

Some public services do, of course, operate in market-like situations. While not exposed to the full rigour of the market in terms of the need to raise revenues to cover costs, leisure centres still need customers, schools pupils, hospitals patients, buses and trains passengers. In these cases, patterns of service use may provide a useful proxy measure of allocative efficiency. A bus without passengers or a library without readers might suggest a misallocation of public resources. But even in concrete instances such as these, it is possible that citizens may value the idea of a library, or the opportunity to use a bus, sufficiently highly to justify the subsidy necessary for their continued operation. That is to say, in public management – even in cases which come close to a market-type exchange – the usual rules of demand and supply do not apply.

Without prices, responsive supply and effective demand there is no automatic process to ensure the allocative efficiency of public services (Samuelson 1954).

Indeed, quite the reverse. It is all too easy for professional providers and politicians to become somewhat divorced from the tax consequences of their performance aspirations. As we explained in chapter two, a large body of theory, albeit sometimes without the accompanying evidence, suggests that government services might be plagued by inefficiency. Governments may then produce the wrong services, in the wrong quantity and at the wrong price (in terms of the taxes or charges that it levies on citizens). So where a service is, in productive terms, provided very efficiently if it is not one that people want or if its supply necessitates what are perceived to be prohibitive levels of taxation, it can still represent an inefficient allocation of resources. That is to say there may be a disjuncture between the goals, processes and performance of public services – as overseen by politicians and professional managers – and the perceptions of those services by citizens.

This chapter does three main things in three sections. In the first, it considers the problem of how to define and measure allocative efficiency. The next section reviews the main institutional mechanisms – voice, choice and process – used by governments to improve allocative efficiency. The third and final section concludes with a discussion of the challenges presented by the allocative efficiency agenda.

Measuring allocative efficiency

Economists distinguish between two aspects of allocative efficiency. The first – focused on the way in which services are supplied – looks 'at the extent to which a firm uses the various factors of production in the best proportions, in view of their prices' (Farrell 1957: 259). Describing this as 'price efficiency', Farrell (1957: 259) says it 'measures a firm's success in choosing an optimal set of inputs'. This chapter, however, is focused on what might be described as the demand-side of allocative efficiency which, in public management, considers citizen satisfaction with the tax-service package provided by the state. In the absence of an invisible hand that ensures allocative efficiency, public managers need a way of determining the optimum tax-service package. Any attempt to change the composition of services or the tax rates necessary to pay for them – to better satisfy citizen expectations – presumes first a capacity to measure satisfaction.

As illustrated in Figure 6.1, the input into the allocative efficiency equation refers to the tax-service package. This consists of the taxes levied on citizens and the manner in which they are spent on the three activities of government – producing services, redistributing resources and investing in capital – we have described in the preceding chapters. In cases where the agency concerned does not have tax-raising powers, it may be that a measure of expenditure will be more appropriate. Governments provide public services, redistribute resources and invest in capital in a bid to solve social problems of one form or another and in such a way deliver the outcome of a satisfied, or at least more satisfied, citizenry. The measurement of allocative efficiency therefore requires

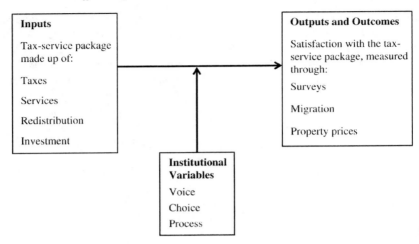

Figure 6.1 Modelling improvements in allocative efficiency.

information on levels of taxation or expenditure *and* levels of satisfaction. Data on inputs and outcomes can be collected separately and then combined. Alternatively, some measures report on overall satisfaction with the combination of inputs and outputs provided by the tax-service package. Either way, allocative efficiency is realized when the combination of inputs and outputs cannot be adjusted in such a way as to increase satisfaction. Four ways of measuring, or at least estimating, allocative efficiency are apparent in the literature: surveys, voice, exit and property prices. We consider each of these in turn.

Surveys

In the absence of the clear signals provided by effective demand, the obvious solution to the problem presented by missing information is of course to ask citizens directly. In such a way, surveys can be used to gauge the level of satisfaction with the package of public services provided by a government (Dowding and Mergoupis 2003). Satisfaction of itself is not, of course, a measure of allocative efficiency, since it makes no reference to tax rates or preparedness to pay.

The input – of taxes or expenditures – can be addressed either by asking respondents specifically about the value for money of the combined tax-service package or by dividing satisfaction by expenditure, or tax, to provide a measure of satisfaction per £. While this methodology does not tell us whether an allo-catively efficient position has been realized, on the assumption that more satisfaction per £ indicates an allocative improvement, it does allow us to compare efficiency performance between public authorities and over time. The same sort of device – in which citizens are asked to indicate incremental changes in the relative priority of different services and tax levels – can be used to gauge an appetite for changes in the tax-service package. In exactly this way, Hills (2002: 542) reports that 'the consistent balance' of respondents in the British Social Attitudes Survey has shown, 'since the late 1980s people have been in favour of higher public spending on "health, education and social benefits"'.

Surveys of citizen opinion are particularly important in areas where public managers are forced to ration services or choose between competing priorities. Bowling (1996: 673) explains that: 'In the context of a lack of adequate knowledge about the costs and effectiveness of much medical care it is important to be democratic and involve everyone in an open debate about rationing.' Based on a random survey of 2005 households, she finds results which suggest that 'the public's priorities are not value free, they are most likely to prioritise treatments specifically for younger rather than older people and particularly lifesaving treatments' (Bowling 1996: 673). In a finding which has implications for our consideration of distributive efficiency in chapter four, she further notes (Bowling 1996: 673) however that 'priorities chosen by the public do not necessarily offer the most equitable solutions in relation to the original aspiration of the NHS of equal treatment for equal need'.

Although superficially attractive, the survey-based approach to the measurement of allocative efficiency is beset by problems which stem from the reliability of citizen assessments. At its simplest, the technique presumes, as Bouckaert and Van de Walle (2003: 331) put it, 'a direct causal relation ... between the quality of a certain service delivery and user satisfaction'. Unfortunately, almost all the work conducted in this area suggests that no such direct causal relationship exists. Indeed, research suggests that the relationship between professional and citizen assessments of service quality varies substantially between services. Van Ryzin, Immerwahr and Altman (2008) find a strong correlation between professional and lay measurements of street cleanliness. Other service areas however 'particularly in areas such as policing' may, as Van Ryzin explains (2007: 528), 'exhibit a poor correspondence between government performance measures and citizen perceptions'. Indeed, some argue that there is no relationship, or even an inverse relationship between the officially measured outputs of public services and levels of citizen satisfaction (Stipak 1979; 1980; Cowell *et al.* 2012; James 2011a).

Evidence of a disjuncture between performance, as measured through managerially defined outputs and citizen satisfaction, underlines the importance of measuring and managing allocative efficiency. It might be said that if citizens are not satisfied by the outputs generated by public service providers, then clearly, governments are producing the wrong outputs. As Van Ryzin (2007: 532) explains, 'traditional performance measures do not necessarily capture the dimensions or features of service quality that matter most to citizens'. Citizens may see and care about different things to professional managers such that 'arrest rates, clearance rates, or even crime rates matter less to citizens than other measures of the safety and security of their neighborhoods, such as loitering, graffiti, and other common indicators of disorder' (Van Ryzin 2007: 528). It would be a mistake, however, to conclude that surveys necessarily provide a reliable measure of the outcomes that matter to citizens. Commentators have suggested a number of different reasons for the disjuncture between performance as measured in terms of public service outputs and outcomes as measured by citizen satisfaction.

First, it is clear that levels of reported satisfaction depend upon the framing of the question. Goodsell (1983) makes the point that citizens' perceptions of public services become more positive when the questions posed to them are more concrete or specific. Bouckaert and Van de Walle (2003: 333) too, report that while citizens may be sceptical in their assessment of government in general, they are more positive in their appraisal of specific services. But then as we have seen, governments do considerably more than provide services. Satisfaction with government presumably reflects an assessment of performance across the three dimensions of services delivery, redistribution and investment together with the tax rates necessary to fund them.

Second, satisfaction appears to depend on the characteristics of the service, as Bouckaert and Van de Walle (2003: 332) explain: 'Frequency of use, homogeneity or heterogeneity of the service and directness of contact with the service all have an influence on customer satisfaction, independent of service quality.' Kelly and Swindell (2002: 274) too, report that: 'Interpersonal contact with service providers appears to be an important element in service satisfaction.'

Third, levels of satisfaction depend also on the characteristics of the respondents and the neighbourhood they live in. De Hoog, Lowery and Lyons (1990) point to a number of relevant variables from ethnicity and wealth to political identification. In their study of levels of satisfaction across 141 spatial areas, Kelly and Swindell (2002: 282) find a negative relationship with minority populations, poverty and residential turnover. Age has less predictable effects with the percentage of the elderly population exhibiting a positive relationship to satisfaction in some services and a negative relationship in others (Kelly and Swindell 2002).

Fourth, satisfaction judgements seem to depend on the prior knowledge and expectations of respondents. The problem, as Deller and Maher (2009: 1187) explain, is that citizens may be 'hard-pressed to judge the validity of service quality claims and typically possess little knowledge about services in other communities'. This can mean as Roch and Poister find (2006: 304) that 'Citizen-consumers report varying levels of satisfaction with services that they perceive to be of similar quality.' Levels of satisfaction will therefore depend on citizens' prior assessment of performance and expectation of what they think it should be. As James (2011b: 1421) describes the problem: 'Models of expectation "confirmation/ disconfirmation" suggest that satisfaction is positively related to performance minus expectations such that higher expectations will be associated with lower satisfaction'; similarly, 'Normative expectations' reflect 'what citizens think performance should be' so that the higher the normative expectations, the lower the satisfaction.

Finally, citizens may use the opportunity presented by satisfaction surveys to wittingly deceive. The problem, as Samuelson (1954: 388–89, emphasis in original) famously explained, is that, 'it is in the selfish interest of each person to give *false* signals, to pretend to have less interest in a given collective consumption activity than he really has'. Or indeed, the reverse may be true, in that respondents may say that they are prepared to pay higher taxes, but then may vote out the political party that imposed them or do their best to avoid paying them.

The relationship between the tax-service package and levels of citizen satisfaction is then far from straightforward. This does not mean, however, that surveys of citizen satisfaction cannot be used in the assessment of allocative efficiency. The many and varied influences on reported satisfaction do suggest though, a danger that surveys can produce skewed results. Citizens may be satisfied or dissatisfied with the tax-service package for a number of different reasons. At the very least, the variables which we now know influence satisfaction – like expectations, service and citizen characteristics – need to be built in as controls to any analysis.

Voice

The social scientist's solution to the response bias of survey-type research is to study actual behaviour. Hirschman (1970) famously argued that consumers confronted with disappointing services could either move to an alternative supplier (the exit option we consider below) or try to voice their complaints with a view to changing the performance of their existing supplier. Sharp (1984: 77) observes that 'among the better-educated … exit is an option of last resort after voice', suggesting that voice may provide a leading indication of migration. The extent to which citizens voice their dissatisfaction with public services can then be taken as an indication of their satisfaction with the tax-service package.

The most venerable way for citizens to exercise voice is of course through the ballot box. It has long been established that voters reward or punish incumbents on the basis of their perceived economic competence (James and John 2007: 568). There is some support too, for the suggestion that tax rates can influence patterns of voting behaviour (James and John 2007: 574). James and John (2007) extend this analysis to the performance of local governments in the UK as publicized through the central inspection system which graded local authorities on their management of key services. They find that 'incumbents with a poor' score 'suffer a 6% loss of support' relative to their reference group (James and John 2007: 574). While poor scores damaged prospects, James and John (2007: 567) found 'no similarly sized reward for those in the highest performance category'. It would seem that the ballot box provides only very broad feedback on the efficiency of the tax-service package.

The opportunity to cast a vote as a summary judgement on a bewildering range of services and issues over an extended period from the past and into the future offers only a very blunt instrument for the expression of satisfaction. Other opportunities to express voice – like referenda – may prove more helpful. In a study of the effect of referenda on tax rates in 26 Swiss Cantons, Feld (1997: 471–72) finds that tax rates for 'high income groups' in Cantons without referenda are 'between seven and nine percent higher than in those cantons with a referendum', a finding consistent with the conclusion that voters use voice to constrain taxes. Similarly, Matsusaka (1995) in the US and Feld and Matsusaka (2003: 2722) in Switzerland, report that jurisdictions 'with direct democracy use their government monies more efficiently'.

Aside from democratic institutions of representative elections and different types of direct democracy, there are a number of other ways in which citizen-service users can voice their dissatisfaction with the tax-service package. Dowding and John (2008) consider two methods. First, dissatisfied citizens can complain individually or privately to the service provider or appeal to some kind of ombudsman or regulatory agency. Alternatively, citizens can express voice collectively by 'joining and campaigning through a pressure group, or signing a petition, going on a march and so on' (Dowding and John 2008: 292). Based on a survey of 4000 UK internet users, they find that 'People are more likely to complain privately about a service when they are dissatisfied' but also 'dissatisfied people are more likely to vote and to engage in other forms of collective participation' (Dowding and John 2008: 306).

Work on these citizen-initiated contacts with government suggest, however, an even more complex pattern of considerations than suggested by satisfaction surveys. Contacts with government are positively associated with awareness, social involvement and political participation (Serra 1995: 184–85). Based on an analysis of Eurobarometer public opinion surveys in 2000 and 2004, Jilke and Van de Walle (2012) find that 'lower educated citizens are less likely to submit a complaint when compared to those with a higher education'. Alongside education, Clifton *et al.* (2013: 8) claim that: 'Complaining is more frequent among men than among women in most of the services and is less frequent among the elderly.' Jilke and Van de Walle (2012) wonder whether 'disadvantaged potentially vulnerable citizens' might emerge as losers in 'two-track' public services in which the more articulate members of the community might negotiate preferential tax-service packages.

With the exception of elections and referenda – where voters are asked to make a summary judgement about the tax-service package – measures of voice need to be combined with some kind of input. This might be the size of the population, the level of public service expenditure, willingness to pay or the level of local tax.

Exit

The third possibility – described by Hirschman (1970) as exit and dubbed by Sharp (1984) as the last resort – occurs when citizens migrate between different tax-service jurisdictions. Tiebout (1956) argued that alongside the mechanisms provided by representative democracy and consumer-type research, citizens could vote with their feet by moving into jurisdictions which strike a better balance between taxation and public service delivery. As Banzhaf and

Walsh (2008: 844) hypothesize: 'neighborhoods that experience an exogenous marginal improvement in public goods' will attract 'relative increases in population density'. They test this hypothesis by looking for population movements coincident with arrival or departure of polluting industry. 'Consistent with the Tiebout model' they find that 'households do appear to vote with their feet in response to changes in public goods' (Banzhaf and Walsh 2008: 844). They report persuasive evidence that migration is indeed correlated with changes in the composition of polluting industries. They further find that the arrival of polluting facilities 'cause[s] the composition of a community to become poorer over time' (Banzhaf and Walsh 2008: 844).

While concerned with public goods in the pure sense of the term, the Banzhaf and Walsh (2008) study is focused on changes in the amenity of the local environment rather than the adequacy of the tax-service package. Feld (1997: 472) engages directly with the tax-service issue, however, in his study of tax rates in Swiss Cantons, concluding that 'high income earners choose their place of residence depending on the amount of income taxes they have to pay'. Based on a survey of 860 respondents who had recently moved house John, Dowding and Biggs (1995) also found support for Tiebout's behavioural assumptions. They conclude that 'Tax-service levels are important, especially as pull factors, as just under half of the respondents consider taxes and/or services an important influence on their choice of new area' (John, Dowding and Biggs 1995: 395). They further find that: 'Respondents who cite Tiebout factors as important are also more likely to move to areas with an improved tax and/or service provision' (John, Dowding and Biggs 1995: 396). Finally, although Dowding and John (2008: 306) 'find only a weak relationship between geographical exit and dissatisfaction' they report that 'Exit from the public to private sectors in education especially, and health, is correlated with dissatisfaction with those services.'

The balance of evidence is more equivocal though. Gill and Rodriguez-Pose's (2012: 178) review of the literature finds some support, balanced against 'an equal number of studies that suggest a weak or non-existent relationship'. Their own analysis of international evidence (Gill and Rodriguez-Pose 2012: 190) suggests only 'a very weak relationship, at best' between 'decentralisation and internal migration'. As they go on to explain, 'the key factors determining the migration decision include differences in opportunities for employment, remuneration rates and quality of life' (Gill and Rodriguez-Pose 2012: 191).

Property prices

Building on Tiebout's insight, other commentators have argued that the patterns of migration and location choice we have described will be capitalized, as the economists put it, into the property prices of the communities affected by these flows. Good schools will for example attract families to the area and in such a way push up house prices (Fack and Grenet 2010; Hilber and Mayer 2009). Reviewing the literature, Nguyen-Hoang and Yinger (2011: 46) report 'extensive evidence that school quality – a public service output – is capitalized into property values'. Despite the different methods adopted in the studies they review, Nguyen-Hoang and Yinger (2011: 46) conclude that they 'provide remarkably similar results, namely that house values rise by 1–4% for a one-standard-deviation increase in student test scores'.

Although the evidence is at its starkest in the matter of school choice, the hypothesis extends to all public services and the levels of tax necessary to pay for them. Indeed, Hilber, Lyytikäinen and Vermeulen (2011: 395) estimate that even central government grants are 'fully capitalized into property values'. Local property prices will, as Oates (1969: 959) famously argued, reflect the trade-off between the range and quality of public services and local taxes such that 'property values would be higher in a community the more attractive its package of public goods'. Testing this theory across Swiss cantons, Feld (1997: 475) finds that 'an increase of the tax burden by 1%…reduces the dwelling rent by 0.37%'. Looking at '169 municipalities in the Swiss metropolitan area of Zurich', Stadelmann (2010: 195) also finds that 'fiscal variables and especially taxes play an important role … Expenditure for culture, health and social well-being determine house prices'.

Property prices offer an attractive measure of allocative efficiency precisely because they appear to reflect, as we have seen, both the quality of local services (and the local environment more broadly defined) *and* the level of local tax rates necessary to pay for them. Brueckner (1982: 311) goes further, arguing that 'if a community's aggregate property value is insensitive to a marginal change in its public good output, then the good is provided at a Pareto efficient level'. In theory then, property prices allow us to go beyond comparisons of relative efficiencies – between organizations or over time – to the identification of an allocatively efficient point at which it is impossible, other things being equal, to improve levels of satisfaction by changing the tax-service package.

Deller and Maher (2009) apply Brueckner's method to the analysis of allocative efficiency in 1830 municipalities in the state of Wisconsin. By calculating the elasticity of property prices they find that 'municipal provided public service levels in Wisconsin are universally under-provided' (Deller and Maher 2009: 1203). Furthermore, by exploring the relationship between prices and different types of expenditure, they are able to suggest which categories of expenditure should be prioritized to improve allocative efficiency in different municipalities. Madison should, for example, increase spending on police, waste and parks but cut back on culture, conservation and community development (Deller and Maher 2009: 1206). Although this fine-grained analysis may lead to managers bolting the stable door after the horse has bolted!

Improving allocative efficiency

Equipped with measures of efficiency, governments can make changes in the tax-service package to deliver allocative improvements. Unfortunately, a formal cycle of research and improvement is unlikely to do the job. Public services, and the expectations of citizens who use them, are too complex and dynamic to be adequately addressed by a linear process of plan–do–check. Rather, if governments are concerned about allocative efficiency then they need to build institutional arrangements which will of themselves lead to improvements in satisfaction.

Advances in productive efficiency of the type considered in chapter three which allow governments to produce more or better services at constant or decreasing cost should lead to improvements in satisfaction. 'Delivering and demonstrating results – producing outcomes that matter to citizens' (Van Ryzin 2011: 746) should perhaps be the first strategy for those who want to improve citizen satisfaction. We have already established, however, that improvements in the efficiency of service production, redistribution and investment, while necessary, are not sufficient for the realization of allocative efficiency. Aside from improving performance in the three dimensions we have already considered, we consider three distinct strategies intended to improve allocative efficiency.

The first reform – we dub the democratic strategy – is guided by the ambition of giving citizens greater voice in service planning through democratic-type reforms. The second – the market strategy – seeks to give citizens greater choice in their consumption of public services. The third – the process strategy – as its name suggests, seeks to improve the processes of service delivery and the way in which citizens are treated by governments. In each case we outline the logic of the different reform strategies before considering evidence, such as it is, of their effectiveness.

Democracy

'Most Americans', according to Hibbing and Theiss-Morse (2001: 152) 'believe governmental processes are inappropriately dominated by elected officials (and the institutions they inhabit) and are insufficiently sensitive to the views of ordinary people'. The democratic strategy is premised on the presumption that if citizens are given greater voice in the planning of public services then the resultant tax-service package will better reflect their wishes. A closer match between the composition of the demand and supply of public services will mean that citizens get what they want and where citizens get what they want, so the argument goes, they will be more satisfied with the tax-service compromise and society will have achieved an improvement in allocative efficiency. There should then be a positive association between opportunities to participate in government decision-making and levels of satisfaction as measured through surveys, migration or property prices. On the basis of analysis of the World Values Survey, Bjørnskov, Dreher and Fischer (2010: 427) find exactly this, suggesting that, 'citizens may derive subjective well-being from having political institutions whenever the bulk of the population has escaped real (absolute) poverty'.

There are a number of different ways of empowering citizens in tax and service planning. First and foremost on the list are reforms intended to improve systems of representative democracy. The advocates of electoral reform argue that preferential electoral systems – which give voters more chance to communicate their preferences for different parties or candidates – make for a more responsive and representative system of government which is better equipped to plan allocatively efficient public services (Lijphart 1999; Anderson and Guillory 1997). In a study of electoral systems and satisfaction across 29 democracies, Farrell and McAllister (2006: 742) find 'firm support for the view that preferential voting can make a difference … such systems promote a greater sense of fairness about election outcomes among citizens, which in turn is a major component of the public's satisfaction with the democratic system'.

Others, however, point to the inherent weaknesses of representative democracy and question whether direct or participative forms of democracy might prove more allocatively efficient. Matsusaka (1995; 2005; 2010) describes direct democracy as the cure of numerous ills. On the basis of an analysis of '10 high-profile issues' determined by 50 states with or without initiative processes (which give voters the power to make direct propositions for new laws) Matsusaka (2010: 135) finds that the match between public preferences and public policies is approximately 18–19% more congruent in initiative than non-initiative states. Feld (1997: 472) also finds that the 'possibility to exert voice in referenda seems to matter' in the location decisions of Swiss citizens. However, based on a comparative analysis of property prices in communities governed through representative and direct democracy in the US state of Maine, Deller and Chicoine (1993: 110) find 'no fundamental difference in the level of allocative efficiency across the two forms of local government'. While in answer to the question do 'state elected officials effectively match policy to local opinion?' Lax and Phillips (2012: 165) report 'clear evidence to the contrary', although they do find that term limits increase 'the probability of congruence by up to 15 percentage points' (Lax and Phillips 2012: 160).

Alongside reforms to the system of democracy, the global trend towards devolution and decentralization is justified on grounds of allocative efficiency (Rodriguez-Pose, Tijmstra and Bwire 2009). Whether through the establishment of new national or regional governments, or through the introduction of community or neighbourhood structures, the guiding thread of these reform strategies is the promise that governments which are closer to the people will govern better. As Rodriguez-Pose, Tijmstra and Bwire (2009: 2043) argue: 'By bringing the government closer to the people, decentralisation may increase citizen participation, transparency, and the accountability of political processes while reducing the costs of collective action and cooperation.' Better systems of participation and accountability should in turn lead to 'a more efficient allocation of public resources, since it both gives the government a better insight into the true preferences of the public and allows for the tailoring of policies to local preferences' (Rodriguez-Pose, Tijmstra and Bwire 2009: 2043).

Based on an analysis of the subjective well-being of 60,000 individuals from 66 countries, Bjørnskov *et al.* (2008: 150) find that people 'clearly benefit from decentralization as measured by the size of local budgets' noting, however, that local autonomy 'increases well-being only insofar as it neutralizes the detrimental impact of the government sector'. Rodriguez-Pose and Maslauskaite (2012: 91) also find that 'citizens increase their level of satisfaction when they perceive they have a greater influence and say over day-to-day policy decisions'. But as Oates explains 'the proper goal of restructuring the public sector cannot simply be de-centralization.' When the governance of almost all countries is realized at multiple levels, the real issue as he goes on to explain 'is one of aligning responsibilities and fiscal instruments with the proper levels of government' (Oates 1999: 1120), a notion we that we consider briefly in chapter eight.

More manageable perhaps than changes to electoral systems or the rescaling of governments are discrete engagement initiatives to raise levels of citizen participation within existing decision-making structures. These can take several forms from simple citizen surveys to deliberative process like juries or partnerships (Lowndes, Pratchett and Stoker 2001). Neshkova and Guo (2012) find that 'greater citizen engagement is strongly and significantly related to better performance of public agencies' although their measures of efficiency are closer to productive than allocative. Critics suggest, however, that to be effective, participation initiatives need to be institutionalized and invested with meaningful powers (Fung and Wright 2001). A thoroughgoing commitment to participation strategies on the part of public organizations may not be much different from the creation of new local layers of government.

Democratic reforms are, though, expensive, both in terms of institutional arrangements required to engage the citizenry, and in terms of the bespoke services they demand. But the democratic agenda is threatened by perhaps a more serious challenge rooted in the citizens' appetite for democratic engagement. While democracy may be good for efficiency, there are limits to the amount of democracy citizens want. Hibbing and Theiss-Morse (2001: 152) explain that although citizens want their governments to be responsive to normal people, they do not necessarily want more democracy.

Choice

For those who think that the prospectus for increased or improved democracy is unrealistic, our second option – of injecting increased choice into public service delivery – may seem more promising. Where public service users are given a choice between different public service providers – or different service options – they should be able to find a service which more closely matches their preferences. A better match of demand and supply, so the theory goes, should yield more satisfaction and improved allocative efficiency.

Over time, and across services, user choices can indicate a preference about where public resources should be allocated. The signals provided by these consumer votes will, however, only improve allocative efficiency if public service providers have the flexibility to respond to these revealed preferences. In simple terms, the flows of money must follow the patterns of citizens' choices. This may mean reallocating resources – from one service to another within an organization – or at a higher level by allowing the organizations providing popular services to expand while letting those organizations providing unpopular services contract or even close. 'The instrumental value of choice' as Dowding and John (2008: 223) explain, 'is that it gives signals for providers that increase both allocative and productive efficiency.'

Choice has been used in a number of different settings across the world. Using data from Minnesota where an open enrolment programme allows school students to transfer from one school district to another, Reback (2005: 279) considers the hypothesis that 'Property values should rise in districts in which the schooling market is strengthened by additional schooling options.' Confirming the hypothesis, he finds that 'A one standard deviation in initial outgoing transfer rates is associated with an increase in house prices of more than three percent' (Reback 2005: 297). Across the state, Reback (2005: 297) concludes, average house prices 'increased due to the adoption of open enrollment' suggesting he argues an 'aggregate welfare gain associated with the weakening of school district boundaries under Minnesota's open enrollment program'. Brunner, Cho and Reback (2012) test the same hypothesis over 12 states with inter-district choice programmes. They too find that a 'moderate expansion of public school choice causes non-trivial changes in households' location patterns and in metropolitan-area housing values' (Brunner, Cho and Reback 2012: 612). 'Our results are consistent', they argue, 'with the prediction that the adoption of an inter-district choice program creates an incentive for relatively high-income households to relocate to previously lower-quality districts to take advantage of lower housing prices' (Brunner, Cho and Reback 2012: 612).

It is relatively easy to specify the institutional arrangements necessary to give parents the power to choose their child's school or, indeed, for patients to choose between different treatment options. But extending choice across the full range of public services is rather more problematic. Choice theorists answer this challenge by proposing the case for competition (and therefore choice) between a number of small governments. As Bates and Santerre (2006: 133) explain, 'The Leviathan theory predicts that more competition among governmental units constrains the excess public spending resulting from monopolistic governments'. They go on to test the theory – while controlling for the productive efficiency advantages of larger size – on data from 169 towns and cities in the US state of Connecticut. Bates and Santerre (2006: 141) find that 'greater efficiency, as reflected in higher property values, occurs in market areas where a relatively large number of equally sized governments exist'.

Dowding and John (2008: 230–31) go on to explain however, that aside from those cases in which 'contracts are relatively easy to specify', choice can impose its own costs and may prove very difficult to evaluate. Clifton *et al.* (2013: 7) warn of a danger that choice-type reforms will benefit 'the middle-class, those with sharper elbows' while it disadvantages the poor, less educated and potentially vulnerable.

Process

So far we have assumed as Ulbig (2002: 793) puts it 'that when people get what they want they do not care how they get it'. But the clear message from all of the work we reviewed in the previous section is that the relationship between the tax-service package and levels of satisfaction is a complicated one. A number of, at first sight, extraneous variables – from the nature of the service to citizen knowledge, expectations and so forth – impact in very important ways on recorded levels of citizen satisfaction. Our third scenario suggests therefore that governments may improve satisfaction levels – and hence allocative efficiency – by targeting these other factors. The process strategy focuses not then on service performance narrowly conceived – in terms of outputs or outcomes – but on the way in which governments deliver services and conduct their business.

In criminal justice, the Thibaut and Walker hypothesis suggests that 'satisfaction with dispute resolution decisions' is independently influenced by 'judgments about the fairness of the dispute resolution process' (Tyler 1988: 103). In the same way that perceptions of procedural justice influence satisfaction in court proceedings, so might the same sorts of consideration influence satisfaction with public services. Developing this line of argument, Van Ryzin (2011: 748) suggests that the way in which governments interact with citizens – and the extent to which citizens perceive those interactions in terms of fairness, equity, respect and honesty – may matter as much as the 'tangible outcomes' measured in traditional approaches to performance management.

Although focused on trust rather than satisfaction, Ulbig (2002: 795) distinguishes between three elements of process which may influence the way in which citizens perceive government. Alongside voice/standing, which we have considered above, she points to the importance of perceived neutrality, equity and honesty in decision-making processes. Citizens also expect, she argues, efficiency and competence in the manner in which governments deal with issues. Based on data from the National Election Survey in the United States, Ulbig (2002: 801) reports that 'satisfaction with the procedures and people of government, in addition to receiving desired policy outcomes, helps to boost feelings of trust in government'. Other studies support this conclusion. Hibbing and Theiss-Morse (2001: 147) start from a premise 'that attitudes toward the processes of government, as apart from the policies, constitute an important, freestanding variable that has serious implications for the health of democracy'. During the course of their focus groups they found that: 'The more we listened' to citizen 'perceptions of government, the more we were taken with the fact that people care deeply about the procedures by which policies are produced' (Hibbing and Theiss-Morse 2001: 147). Grimes (2006: 306) too, finds that process matters. Arguing that 'opportunities to influence the decision outcome are not a crucial component in institutional trust' but that 'citizens' consent to authority hinges upon perceived propriety in decision processes' (Grimes 2006: 303). Similarly Tolbert and Mossberger (2006: 356) report that 'citizens base their evaluations on *process* considerations ... how fair, open, and responsive political and governmental processes are'. Based on a survey of 690 residents of Lincoln, Nebraska, Herian *et al.* (2012: 829) find that 'Process fairness will positively impact overall evaluations of government and policy support represented by the perceived value of tax dollars.' Finally, based on an analysis of data from the international social survey programme, Van Ryzin (2011: 755) finds support for his hypothesis concluding that 'the effect of process on trust appears larger – in some cases several times larger – than the effect of outcomes on trust'.

While citizen perceptions of process seem to matter, it is not clear, as Grimes (2006: 290) suggests, how 'political institutions and the individuals who work within them' can improve perceptions of process. Considerable hope has been invested in the possibility that the adoption of developments in information and communication technologies may allow governments to get closer to citizens. Findings are, though, mixed. Based on a sample of 815 government website users in the US, Tolbert and Mossberger (2006: 366) find that 'E-government at the local level' was perceived as 'making government accessible and responsive', and that 'visiting a local government Web site led to enhanced trust in local government, controlling for other attitudinal and demographic factors'. However, focused on satisfaction and trust in US federal government, Morgeson and Petrescu (2011: 467) find that 'easily obtainable and timely and efficient services are most vital in determining citizen satisfaction' but that 'egovernment usage' has a 'significant but negative effect'.

Conclusion

Allocative efficiency is difficult to measure but it is perhaps even more difficult to prescribe the institutional changes which will improve it. But it is nonetheless, the most important dimension of efficiency we consider in this book. In the long run, there really is no point in governments producing goods and services, redistributing resources or investing in different types of capital if those activities are not valued by citizens.

When politicians and citizens are on the same page, the allocative efficiency agenda will sit comfortably with the productive, distributive and dynamic efficiency agendas. More formally, with a good correlation between traditional measures of performance – developed by politicians and managers – and satisfaction as established through citizen surveys or patterns of migration, all the usual techniques of performance improvement (Ashworth, Boyne and Entwistle 2010) will garner improvements in allocative efficiency. In such a way, advances in productive efficiency – which allow more people to be treated in hospital per unit of tax – can also be expected to increase citizen satisfaction. Different perceptions of the relative importance of the different activities of government can produce a significant disjuncture between the different dimensions of performance. Indeed given the varied makeup of the citizen body in liberal democracies – from, on the one hand, those who are dependent on services but pay no taxes, to those who pay taxes but make little call on services – maintaining high levels of satisfaction across the different dimensions of government activity is an achievement indeed.

Circumstances like these suggest that more attention needs to be paid to improving the signals or lines of communication between citizens and managers. There is evidence to suggest that the reforms we have discussed – in terms of voice, choice and process – can play an important part in improving these signals, in turn, raising satisfaction with government. The literature does not tell us, however, which of these strategies promises the best value for money. We just do not know whether a government keen to improve citizen satisfaction should focus on choice, voice or process. We do know, however, that all three reform strategies require costly institutional change of one form or another. Whether the return on those investments represents good value for money or better value than an investment in one of the other dimensions of efficiency we have considered is a question to which we now turn.

7 Managing for efficiency in a democracy

In the previous chapters, we discussed our four faces of public service efficiency in some depth, reflecting on the ways in which they have been conceptualized, measured and pursued by governments across the globe. For the purposes of conceptual and empirical clarity, the arguments that we developed were very much focused on the particular dimension of efficiency under consideration; we did not consider the consequences of policies to promote one dimension of efficiency for each of the other dimensions in any detail. Yet, the conceptual and practical questions about measuring and managing productive, distributive, dynamic and allocative efficiency cannot be addressed in isolation from each other, especially within a properly functioning democracy. Given the multiple values inherent in democratic public administration, the 'market' for policy ideas and management strategies concerned with the pursuit of public service efficiency is unlikely to exist in 'perfect' equilibrium for long at any given point in time. Hence, decisions about the relative priority accorded to each of the different dimensions of efficiency – both within and across time – are an inescapable feature of the challenge of managing public service efficiency. At the same time, these decisions are made in public and so the rationale for making one set of choices rather than another must have a firm foundation.

That there are multiple perspectives on the ways in which the efficiency of public services might be improved signals that the evaluation of policy interventions intended to enhance efficiency is as important as the arguments made on behalf of those interventions. The publicness of public services places a great onus on policy-makers and public managers to be transparent in their decision-making, and, this in turn, indicates that they should be held to account for upholding certain standards of public justification for the policy positions that they adopt. For public administration scholars, the demand for transparency and accountability is the source of the moral authority that underpins the state provision of public goods and the public value that public services create (Moore 1995). For political theorists, the requirement that public policy and management decisions be justified to the citizenry is characteristic of the public philosophy of democratic government (Weale 2011). In fact, though we disagree with Dwight Waldo's banishment of efficiency from the public administration lexicon, we are in agreement with him on the vital role that political theory can play in helping to clarify the enterprise of democratic public administration.

In previous chapters, we drew upon political theory to illustrate the inherently normative character of the efficiency challenge, especially the theories of distributive justice that can shape the pursuit of distributive efficiency. In thinking about the role that public justification might play in managing for efficiency in a democracy, we can turn to John Rawls' (1996) ideas about public reason for inspiration. Public reason can be broadly defined as the guiding normative ideal behind theories of deliberative democracy. It presupposes that participants in democratic deliberation should appeal to the public good rather than their private interests by justifying their proposals 'on the basis of mutually acceptable reasons' (Gutmann and Thompson 1996: 55). The concept of public reason thus has obvious relevance for the theory and practice of democratic public administration, since these are explicitly concerned with the extent to which organizations create 'public value' rather than private profit or gain (Moore 1995). According to Rawls, public reason ensures that the:

> structure of government be changed only as experience shows it to be required by political justice or the general good, and not as prompted by the political advantage of one party or group that may at the moment have the upper hand
>
> (Rawls 1996: 224–28)

As a guide to the conduct of democratic public administration, the concept of public reason can therefore represent an ethical ideal to which politicians, policy-makers and public managers should aspire when explaining the rationales behind the decisions that they make. It can, moreover, provide a strong philosophical basis for the pursuit of evidence-based policy-making. Indeed, wide-ranging debate and research concerned with improving public service efficiency would serve as a powerful regulative ideal for the practical conduct of democratic politics and administration (Bohman 1999; Weale 2011). When managing for efficiency in a democracy, the measurement and evaluation of productive, distributive, dynamic and allocative efficiency is therefore a principle of government; and one which implies the varying effects of interventions on each efficiency dimension be debated.

The democratic foundations of public administration impose constraints on the choices that can be made between different dimensions of public service efficiency, and the range of policies that might lead to efficiency gains. At the same time, adherence to an ideal of public reason also opens up the opportunity for creative policy-making and management aimed at delivering tangible benefits for taxpayers, citizens and other stakeholders in ways that can be publicly justified. Although trade-offs between different dimensions may be necessary, it is conceivable that they can be justified in ways that reflect the ideal of public reason. In this chapter, we identify those efficiency scenarios we believe are most likely to be encountered by policy-makers and public managers charged with improving the management of efficiency. We elaborate on the broad empirical realities that typify those scenarios and how they might be managed. Thereafter, we offer some thoughts on how the management of the multiple dimensions of efficiency can be best evaluated (and publicly justified). In doing so, we draw upon case studies of the UK experience of four key efficiency focused policies to illustrate the importance of efficiency evaluation in democratic public administration.

Public sector efficiency scenarios

The arguments developed in this book raise numerous important theoretical and practical questions about the relationships between the different dimensions of efficiency that require more extended consideration. It is not the purpose of this chapter to address all of the possible permutations of fit and misfit between the policies designed to improve productive, distributive, dynamic and allocative efficiency. Rather we seek to explore some of the broader issues that confront policy-makers and public managers as they grapple with the efficiency problem. The account of efficiency derived from the theory of perfect competition suggests that each of the different dimensions are compatible, indeed, necessary for the achievement of economic and social efficiency. However, as we have sought to illustrate throughout the book, within the public sector, there is no automatic process which ensures that the productive, distributive, dynamic and allocative efficiency of public service operations will be in harmony. In fact, in some circumstances, it is quite possible that the different dimensions of efficiency will be brought into conflict as the demands of attaining improvements in one may have negative implications for another. All of which underlines that public service efficiency needs to be measured, managed and evaluated by politicians and public officials.

In seeking to improve public service efficiency, policy-makers and public managers cannot be guided solely by the Pareto condition which requires that someone can only be made better off if no-one else is made any worse off. There is, of course, merit in seeing Pareto optimality as a starting-point rather than the end-point for the redistribution of the costs and benefits of public service production, as Grandy (2009) emphasizes. However, the concept of public service efficiency is inherently contestable, as too are the alternative approaches to its measurement and management. Since normative concerns inform stakeholders' views about the appropriate means for measuring, managing and improving efficiency, there is an on-going need to be sensitive to the public justification of policies designed to meet the efficiency challenge, especially in the case of the distributive and dynamic dimensions. Those policies should also be a good fit with the context in which they are being applied, particularly in terms of the ways in which they accommodate the intertwining of each dimension of efficiency. In fact, in this chapter we argue that it is possible to discern three broad overarching efficiency scenarios that are the likely result of that intertwining.

Everyone's a winner

Like the theory of perfect competition, our first scenario sees the four dimensions we have described as compatible or harmonious parts of a greater efficiency. In the absence of market competition, citizens' demands – communicated through the democratic system – will ensure that the state provides the right services, in the most efficient way, distributing them both between groups and over time so as to maximize welfare. To ensure that efficiency is achieved, the task of the policy-maker is simply to operationalize the priorities signalled by the representatives of the electorate; the job of the public manager is to implement policy with as little fuss as possible, tweaking things here and there to meet local circumstances. Governments which fail to listen to the signals from their citizens, or fail to implement their directives as efficiently as possible will be punished at the ballot box. Likewise, the management of those public services that fail to successfully adapt voter-approved policies to client needs is likely to be scrutinized with greater vigour.

In theory, properly functioning democratic systems are intrinsically geared towards delivering efficient solutions to social needs – as well as other public values that do not fall under the rubric of efficiency. Certainly, allocative efficiency is only likely to be improved where this is the case, but there may be good reason to anticipate that the other dimensions of efficiency will benefit from a close alignment between policies for their advancement and the values espoused by the electorate. After all, the shared values of a society are what underpin its acceptance of the tax burden associated with producing public services (Easton 1965). Within this 'everyone's a winner' scenario, managing for efficiency in a democracy is essentially guaranteed via the strength of the connections between political institutions and the bureaucracy; or, more specifically, the quality of the relationships between politicians and bureaucrats. Where politicians are able to accurately interpret and respond to the signals from voters, and, in turn, are able to shape bureaucrats' values and preferences in their own image, one might anticipate that each dimension of efficiency is more likely to be both pursued and realized.

The demands of managing this efficiency scenario may seem to place undue pressure on the political system and the bureaucracy to be responsive to the wishes of the median voter, whose representativeness of the citizenry as a whole can be called into question. That is, expecting democracy to function as a surrogate for perfect economic competition may be theoretically appealing but is practically implausible, especially when the real world is replete with examples of politicians rigging the game for electoral benefit at significant social cost (e.g. Ward and John 1999). Yet, there are examples of governments achieving efficiency 'win–wins' in practice that offer at least some hope that a virtuous efficiency circle can be achieved. For instance, Denmark benefits from some of the best quality public services in the world, exhibits very low levels of social inequality and government indebtedness, and is home to the happiest people on the planet (Campbell and Pedersen 2007). Still, such cases of success across the board are unlikely to be the norm in as contested a field as the management of public services.

On balance, it seems more intuitive to expect there to be significant trade-offs to be made between the different dimensions of efficiency, particularly when one considers that the values shared by citizens may be minimal at best (Gray 2000). Or, put differently, very few countries are as socially homogenous and cohesive as Denmark and the other Scandinavian states. In fact, many political theorists argue that value incommensurability is now the norm in contemporary liberal democracies (e.g. Raz 1986; Gray 2000). This implies that the attribution of value to the pursuit of any one particular good inevitably implies a corresponding loss, because for individuals and societies it is impossible to pursue all possible goods simultaneously, an insight that lies at the heart of our second efficiency scenario.

Someone has to lose

In stark contrast to our first efficiency scenario, our second scenario envisages fundamental tensions and inevitable trade-offs between the different dimensions of efficiency. Strategies to maximize productive efficiency may have the effect of standardizing services to the point where there is a poor match between the kind of services valued by citizens and those which are provided (Billis and Glennerster 1998). Similarly, a focus on allocative efficiency points towards the devolution of responsibilities to smaller organizations better placed to provide bespoke or targeted public services, albeit with the attendant danger that one community's bespoke service is likely to be perceived as another's 'postcode lottery'. Moreover, the introduction of systems which facilitate choice between public service providers may bring gains in allocative efficiency but the increased cost of administering such a system may result in losses in productive efficiency. Likewise a focus on the distributive dimension might prioritize particular groups with disproportionate levels of need, but, in turn, require considerable investment in the development of organizational capabilities sufficient to identify and address these needs effectively. Finally, a focus on efficiency over time suggests early and preventative type interventions and investments to head off future problems, but also implies that current priorities may be neglected in favour of projected ones whose potential tractability may be uncertain.

On this reading of the efficiency challenge, determining how the trade-offs between different dimensions of efficiency can be justified is the stock-in-trade of politicians and policy-makers. Democratic public administration is then essentially the working out of the messy organizational realities associated with the politics of who gets what, when and how, rather than a well-oiled machine for the perfect communication of the electorate's preferences in to public service production. In fact, tensions between the different dimensions of efficiency will, according to this second scenario, likely be compounded rather than resolved by the democratic process which signals only the electorate's desire to have high public spending *and* low taxation, personalized services yet uniform standards, equal rights *and* responsibilities, and high quality services 'from the cradle to the grave'. All of which suggests that the task of meeting the efficiency challenge in a democracy is more complicated, resource-intensive and fraught with political danger than was implied in our first scenario. For democratic public administration to function effectively, the bureaucracy is therefore likely to play an especially active role in steering the process by which the tensions between the different stakeholders in the provision of public services are resolved.

The problem of interpreting and implementing the conflicting and contradictory goals of the citizenry is taken up by political parties when they develop policies for inclusion in their election manifestos. However, the tensions inherent in making decisions about which dimension of public service efficiency to prioritize are as often made by the bureaucrats responsible for putting political programmes into practice. The management and steering of the politics of public services typically occurs on an incremental basis, reflecting the need to work with the multiple stakeholders involved in addressing the efficiency problem as effectively as possible (Quinn 1980). This work does not occur in an administrative vacuum. Rather it is likely to be conducted in the face of very serious conflicts between competing managerial and political priorities. Public justification of the decisions resulting from the process of stakeholder management is thus a key feature of democratic public administration within this scenario, in a way that it need not be within the first efficiency scenario.

In our second scenario, the relative emphasis laid on productive, distributive, dynamic and allocative efficiency is in many ways a function of the skills and strategies of those public managers and professionals who have to navigate their way through the minefield of contested public purposes (Hoggett 2006). To negotiate these conflicts, public managers may do best to develop what negotiation scholars describe as 'integrative solutions' that identify 'zones of possible agreement' between competing priorities with a view to ascertaining those solutions most likely to deliver the greatest joint if differential gains (Lax and Sebenius 1987). Such solutions too may be more susceptible to the condition of public justification than those which simply assert that 'well, someone has to lose'. The success with which public managers do this will in large part be dependent upon the practical craft and experience that they can bring to the task (Mintzberg 2004). The impact of such contingent organizational factors on the prospects of efficiency improvement is thus an important consideration when reflecting on the development and design of appropriate policies, and it is the element of contingency that is at the heart of our final efficiency scenario.

Win some, lose some

Our last scenario suggests a combination of the first two such that the compatibility of the different dimensions of efficiency will depend upon the design of policies and strategies. Although each dimension of efficiency is typically associated with particular policies and reform approaches – productive efficiency with bureaucratic prescriptions for mergers and standardization for example – there isn't a single true path to the realization of one or other dimension of efficiency. Some policies may prove more efficacious than others in improving efficiency and different policies may well present alternative patterns of compatibility or incompatibility between each of the different dimensions of efficiency. According to our third scenario, the achievement of efficiency depends not upon the dimension of efficiency but on the intended (and unintended) effects of the specific policies adopted to advance particular dimensions. In this scenario, the formal processes through which policymakers develop strategies to realize efficiency and the quality of policy design are what matters rather than the working of the democratic system or the skill with which bureaucrats 'muddle through' contested terrain.

In theory, formal decision-making processes hold out the possibility that the divergent effects of alternative policies and strategies can be brought into harmony through rational analysis and planning. A further advantage of rational processes of policy design is that they can be tailored to address the established weaknesses of existing initiatives, and of existing provision in the case of public services (Moore 1995). Or, in other words, that targets for improvement can be set that reflect the scale and scope of the efficiency problem for different public services. Indeed, through techniques such as options appraisal, cost–benefit analysis and logic modelling, it is possible that policymakers and public managers can improve the design of initiatives to such an extent that the win–win situation elaborated in our first efficiency scenario is obtained through strategic planning rather than institutional design. Bryson (2010: 255) contends that such planning 'typically "works" and often works extremely well' because it brings together all of the important elements of public management; and, the available evidence on the issue tends to support this conclusion (Boyne 2010b). Still, little empirical research on this topic has actually addressed the potential unintended consequences of rational planning (though see Kelman and Friedman 2009).

Equally likely, in theory and in practice, is the possibility that planning processes, however effective for improving policy design, are unable to deliver improvements across multiple dimensions of public service performance. This may be especially so for the four dimensions of efficiency, given that the financial constraints gains on one dimension might impose on gains in the others. In fact, no matter how well planned and designed, it is unlikely that any one policy or initiative will deliver uniform benefits for each dimension of efficiency for a whole host of reasons. Even so, when reflecting on the impact of any given policy on efficiency, it is the overall efficiency gains and losses that should be studied and evaluated, as it is only by doing so that the requirement that public reason be focused on the good of the public as a whole can be met (Rawls 1996).

Summing up: evaluating overall efficiency gains and losses

Evaluation of the overall gains and losses on each of the dimensions of public service efficiency is not only something that would be a requirement of public reason, it can also reveal which of the alternative efficiency scenarios seems to have prevailed in the wake of policy change. To sum up the impact of any given policy or initiative and assess which of our scenarios appears to have emerged from the intervention, it is necessary to bring together information about productive, distributive, dynamic and allocative efficiency. To make this task manageable, an overall efficiency evaluation could draw upon information that is very narrowly defined and tightly linked to the specific features of an intervention (e.g. input–output analysis) or that is very broad in its scope (e.g. ratings scores, meta-analytical techniques). Either way, when seeking to sum up gains and losses it will be important to find some way of combining the measures of each dimension of efficiency that accords each an equivalent degree of relevance and importance.

In the foregoing chapters we explored how each dimension of efficiency might be measured with some degree of precision using relevant input and output indicators, and explored the applicability of a balanced scorecard. Whereas the balanced scorecard approach might be especially useful for large-scale government-led reforms and interventions, the impact of the smaller-scale initiatives undertaken by public organizations and managers could be evaluated with some precision using only input and output data. This approach would prove especially useful if indicators were available that captured inputs that were common to the pursuit of productive, distributive, dynamic and allocative efficiency, and that could then be brought together with relevant bespoke output indicators for each efficiency dimension. It might then be possible to use analytical techniques that can determine the impact of a policy change on each dimension of efficiency simultaneously, such as Seemingly Unrelated Regression or Structural Equation Modelling.

Figure 7.1 presents a schematic representation of a Structural Equation Model analysing the hypothetical impact of a new customer service training programme on customer satisfaction with the work of a large welfare services office. Labour replacement costs associated with receiving the training and the costs of employing the trainers could be used as indicators of the inputs. Data from a survey of the staff within the organization carried out before and after the intervention could be used to assess changes in output quantity and quality, customer satisfaction, equality of access and levels of human capital within the organization. The impact of the training programme itself could be measured by asking staff whether or not they had received the training. The impact of the intervention on total costs per unit of service delivered would square the efficiency circle.

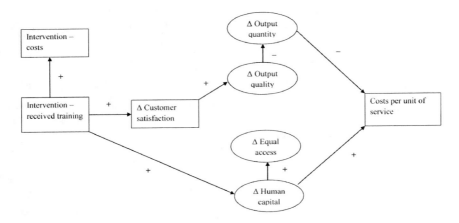

Figure 7.1 Structural Equation Model of the hypothetical impact of customer service training on changes ($\triangle$) in efficiency.

According to our hypothetical example, a direct positive effect is observed between receiving customer service training and customer satisfaction, with an indirect positive effect observed for the quality of service mediated by the improvement in satisfaction. An indirect negative effect is also observed for the quantity of service provided, mediated by the improvement in service quality. The training itself has a direct effect on the indicator of dynamic efficiency, but no relationship with that for distributive efficiency. These results are therefore indicative of the third efficiency scenario, which posits that there may be unintended effects associated with policy change, in this hypothetical case, the reduction in output quantity, which may (or may not), in turn, need to be remedied through a subsequent intervention.

As well as introducing a range of relevant input and output indicators that could be drawn upon to conduct very precise analyses of policy interventions, we developed an efficiency balanced scorecard in chapter three as a way of bringing together and simplifying information on stakeholders' perceptions of inputs and outputs. This approach offers an indication of the ways in which it might be possible to explore the broad impact of a policy on different dimensions of efficiency goals and on different stakeholders. So, for instance, one could tally up efficiency scores or ratings by dimension or by stakeholder group, and present this information in a tabular format.

Table 7.1 illustrates a potential efficiency scenario that results from the hypothetical forced merger of a set of local governments. By efficiency dimension, it is clear that gains across the different dimensions of efficiency are extremely variable, and that considerable losses may actually have been incurred as a result of the intervention. This assessment can be extended further by stakeholder, which suggests that the only winners are central government

Table 7.1 Balanced scorecard for hypothetical local government amalgamation

Efficiency dimension	Stakeholders in Public Service Efficiency			
	Service users	Professionals	Councillors/Managers	Government
Inputs	Local tax payable	Total hours worked	Total budget	Grant allocation
Productive	Service quality unchanged	Organizational commitment weakened	Administrative savings offset by transition costs	Strategic management at local level strengthened
Distributive	Perceived fairness of service distribution worsened	Public service motivation unchanged	Tensions between senior people from reallocation of roles and responsibilities	Grant distribution simplified
Dynamic	Life satisfaction unchanged	Perceived job insecurity higher	Reserves used to cover transition costs	Long-term local government costs stabilised
Allocative	Transparency of decision-making improved	Job satisfaction weakened	Citizen voice more diffused	Popular support for action to make savings

officials, and that while citizens seem unconcerned, local politicians and council staff are clear losers. The pattern of findings therefore follows much of the established empirical literature on local government amalgamation, and is therefore suggestive of the second efficiency scenario advanced above, i.e. that someone has to lose.

These alternative approaches to summing up the efficiency gains and losses can be used to paint more or less detailed pictures of the efficiency scenarios that emerge from policy interventions. They can also be used to derive scenarios from the evidence of past interventions, which in itself is an important feature of the policy evaluation process that should not be ignored. To illustrate the relevance of backward-looking evaluations, we devote the remainder of the chapter to the analysis of four real-world efficiency case studies using the available evidence to depict the scenarios resulting from government action on efficiency and the challenges and opportunities these provide for the public justification of policies to improve efficiency.

Efficiency case studies

The management of efficiency in a democracy requires more than simply juggling the claims of different groups. To address the efficiency problem in the public sector, there needs to be a conscious effort to make improvements happen on the part of policy-makers and public managers. However, it is clear from the policies associated with the different dimensions of efficiency that a strategy designed to improve performance in one dimension isn't necessarily compatible with the advancement of another. Although the outcome of policy and management change is invariably messy and contested, it is entirely plausible that each of the three scenarios that we describe above might emerge in the wake of an efficiency-orientated intervention. They may even co-exist to some extent, where, for example, improvements on all four dimensions of efficiency are the result of policy action, but one of the dimensions sees much more dramatic improvement than the others.

To illustrate the ways in which the alternative efficiency scenarios have actually arisen in the wake of policy change, we now explore some real-world UK case studies documenting the overall efficiency impact of policies and initiatives that were designed with one specific dimension of efficiency in mind. To do so, we begin by describing the initiatives and reflect on their likely efficiency implications, before mapping what is known about those implications in tabular format. We start with the contracting out of public services in the UK as perhaps the paradigmatic example of a policy intended to improve productive efficiency. Next, the impact of the devolution of a measure of political power from the UK government to Wales in 1998 is assessed as an example of a policy for improving allocative efficiency. Following that, we examine the New Deal for Communities initiative that was aimed at improving distributional efficiency by regenerating some of the most deprived neighbourhoods in England's cities. Finally, the overall efficiency impact of Private Finance Initiatives on UK public services is evaluated.

Contracting out

The tensions between the different dimensions of efficiency are very clearly played out in theories of contracting out in the public sector. As we have seen, efforts to involve the private sector in the provision of public services are driven by the economics of incentives. From this perspective, the introduction of contestability and competition within the market for public services makes it possible for government to capture some of the economic efficiency of the free market. That is, that where there is free competition for the provision of public services, costs will be driven down and productivity driven upwards as firms compete for business. At the same time, the direct involvement of the private sector in public services can bring positive externalities in the shape of new knowledge, innovation and managerial capability that can be shared with the commissioning agency. These arguments are hugely contested, ideological even (Studlar, MacAllister and Ascui 1990), but continue to shape the discourse around the contracting's efficiency effects.

Contracting out is particularly popular amongst governments seeking to cut the size and cost of the public sector (Feigenbaum, Henig and Hamnett 1998). Advocates invariably point to the gains in productive efficiency likely to result from competition between the firms bidding to provide public services. However, those stakeholders concerned about distributive efficiency baulk at the prospect of private firms being responsible for providing public services to those in most need of them. Stakeholders concerned with efficiency over time have suggested that any short-term gains in productive efficiency may dissipate over the long term, as initial profits gradually decline and contractors become unwilling to meet the structural costs associated with long-term provision (Parker and Hartley 2003). Finally, stakeholders focused on the allocative dimension argue that business does a better job of meeting customer demands, and so, in theory, contracting out may result in an improved connection between what the public wants and what it gets.

Welsh devolution

Aside from the argument from first principles in favour of Welsh self-government, the devolution of powers from Westminster to Cardiff was based on a very straightforward argument about improved allocative efficiency. Since Welsh politicians and officials are better placed than national policy-makers to understand and respond to the particular needs and aspirations of Wales, it makes sense to grant them the powers and resources to develop localized policy solutions (Keating 1998). In fact, pro-devolutionists touted the need for policies tailored to the particular socio-economic and political circumstances of Wales (Bradbury 2003); and, in the wake of devolution, Welsh politicians and policy-makers strove to develop a distinctive policy agenda that better reflected the left-leaning political preferences of the electorate in Wales (Bradbury 2005). Examples of what the then leader of the Welsh Government described as 'clear red water' between Cardiff and Westminster (Morgan 2002) included policies subsidized by the government with a view to enhancing distributive efficiency: free prescriptions, free breakfasts for school children, and free swimming for those under 16 and over 60.

Allied to the development of bespoke distributional policies was a very different approach to the issue of productive efficiency. In a bid to assert the distinctiveness of a Welsh policy agenda, many of the core policies for improving public service efficiency in England, such as competition, choice and performance management were rejected by policy-makers in Wales, and much greater emphasis was placed upon joint production. In terms of productive efficiency, then, fewer tools for its improvement were being applied, whilst the bare fact of devolution was assumed to ensure allocative efficiency. By supplementing UK-wide tax-and-spend policies with distributional initiatives, distributive efficiency may be improved. In terms of dynamic efficiency, prior studies suggest subnational governments have little incentive to exercise fiscal discipline (Rodden 2002), and so short-term political concerns can supersede long-term investment plans.

New Deal for Communities

The New Deal for Communities (NDC) programme was a large-scale area-based initiative launched by the UK Labour government in 1998 to address urban deprivation in the cities of England. The NDC was designed to reduce the gap between the social and economic outcomes in the most deprived urban neighbourhoods and the rest of England. Thirty-nine partnerships were set up and given a budget of approximately £50 million to deliver a ten-year improvement plan in relation to six key outcomes: crime, community, housing, education, health and worklessness (Lawless 2011). The NDC programme therefore clearly represents a scheme that was implemented with a view to improving the distributive efficiency of public services, though its long-term approach also indicates that it was intended to enhance dynamic efficiency through investment in the physical, human and social capital in deprived areas.

The NDC was a flagship policy for the Labour government, and it was hoped that the scale of investment would result in long-lasting change in those areas experiencing socio-economic disadvantage. Such positive change was anticipated to show up in improvements in the kinds of indicators of output quality and citizen satisfaction discussed in chapters three and six, and was expected to occur at a faster rate than for elsewhere in England. The programme incorporated large-scale national evaluations of the first phase of the NDC (2001–5) and its second phase (2006–10). As well as drawing lessons about the management and organization of the NDC programme, these evaluations were charged with examining changes in local outcomes on the basis of statutory performance indicators and a bespoke survey (Foden, Grimsley, Lawless and Wilson 2010). The NDC therefore represents an especially striking example of a distributional policy with specific aims and objectives whose success can be investigated with some rigour.

Private Finance Initiative

Like the NDC, Private Finance Initiative (PFI) represents an excellent example of a policy with a very clear efficiency goal, in this case the long-term efficiency of the public sector. More specifically, PFI has been encouraged as a means for ensuring the dynamic efficiency of capital-intensive areas of the public sector, especially the physical infrastructure supporting public services, such as schools, hospital, roads and other transportation projects. PFI schemes were initially developed by the UK Conservative government in the 1990s, but came to be associated with the Labour government of the 2000s. The use of PFIs has since become popular in numerous other OECD countries (Greve and Hodge 2010). A good example of a large-scale PFI scheme in the UK context is the Building Schools for the Future Programme introduced by the Labour government in 2006, which was intended to renew the entire stock of English secondary schools, but was subsequently terminated by the Coalition government in 2010.

Although the economic rationale behind their use is akin to that which lies behind contracting out and privatization, PFIs have been applied with a much more specific purpose in mind than simply reducing the costs of producing a public service. Rather, their use has been encouraged as a means to enable public services to make investments in capital infrastructure that would not be possible without private sector involvement. This is not necessarily the cheapest of the alternative approaches to managing the capital infrastructure of the public sector, but in the context of tight fiscal rules, PFIs offer a means for making investments happen that would not otherwise occur. This suggests that while dynamic efficiency might receive a boost from the use of PFIs, productive efficiency may suffer, particularly given the transaction costs associated with making public–private partnerships work (Parker and Hartley 2003). In terms of allocative efficiency, it would seem likely that service users and public officials will prefer new shiny facilities to dilapidated ones. Improvements in distributive efficiency may be less certain due to the potential for private investors to cream off excessive profits through the sale of equity shares.

Mapping the case studies

To illustrate the efficiency effects of the four policies discussed above, we present the results of a mapping exercise in Table 7.2 that assesses the balance of the evidence on the merits of those policies for each dimension of efficiency. A multitude of studies were undertaken in the 1980s and 1990s analysing the

Table 7.2 Efficiency case studies

Efficiency dimension	Policies for Improving Efficiency			
	Contracting out	Welsh Devolution	New Deal for Communities	Private Finance Initiatives
Productive	Balance of empirical evidence suggests cost savings, but deteriorations in quality.	Performance of Welsh public services generally worse than those in England, especially schools, hospitals and ambulance services	Monetized benefits outweigh costs for perceived quality of life. Open question whether improvements in output quality are cost-effective.	Improvements in output quality, but increased transaction costs and running costs.
Distributive	Service provision not based on need, with contractors preferring more profitable and less costly clientele.	Increased uptake of beneficial activities amongst low-income and harder-to-reach groups.	Improvements on some indicators for most deprived groups (e.g. employment rates), also for inclusiveness of governance in terms of gender and ethnicity.	Gains in equity for private shareholders, taxpayers footing bill for PFI failures.
Dynamic	Cost-savings in the short-term, but increased monitoring costs in the long run.	Capital investment not a priority. Short-term electoral advantage based on policies intended to improve allocative and distributive efficiency	Most deprived neighbourhoods remain in a similar predicament to that they were in prior to the intervention.	New infrastructure in place, but costs of repayment extremely high and causing bankruptcy in some cases.
Allocative	Mixed evidence on customer satisfaction.	Welsh public much happier with standard of public services than English. Successful referendum for further extension of powers.	Satisfaction with some services improved. No evidence of declining satisfaction.	Public professionals are satisfied with new buildings, but examples of over-supply of new schools.
Overall verdict	Delivers on promise of productive efficiency gains, but probably at the expense of other dimensions of efficiency (scenario 2)	Delivered on promise of allocative efficiency gains. Negative and positive unintended effects on the other dimensions of efficiency. (scenario 3)	Delivered on promise of distributive efficiency gains. Mixed effects on the other efficiency dimensions (scenario 3)	Delivered on promise of more and better outputs, but negative unintended effects for three dimensions of efficiency (scenario 2)

impact of contracting out on productive efficiency in UK public services. Although the methodological rigour of many of these studies can be questioned (Boyne 1998), the evidence suggests that contracting out and privatization tended to result in cost-savings, at least, in the short term (Domberger and Jensen 1997). However, more recently evidence has been mounting of the transaction costs associated with monitoring and managing private suppliers (e.g. Entwistle 2005; Lonsdale *et al.* 2010). Research has also found that service quality in the NHS, in particular, may deteriorate where contracting out is more prevalent (Davies 2010); and there is some cross-sectional evidence from English local government to suggest that perceptions of service equity, responsiveness and value for money may also suffer (Andrews and Van de Walle 2013). Although other research has suggested that recipients of domiciliary care and employment services provided by firms are more satisfied (National Consumer Council 2007), more research on users' experience of contracted services would be extremely valuable. In addition, the transparency of corporate reporting and financial practice in large private providers of UK public services remains a particular problem (Hood, Fraser and McGarvey 2006). Overall, then there appears to be considerable scope for more systematic research in this area, especially as private firms account for such large swathes of UK public expenditure (Julius 2008).

The impact of policy divergence in Wales on public services has been the subject of a number of studies. Most of this work has compared the performance of public services in Wales with those in England (e.g. Andrews and Martin 2010; Burgess, Wilson and Worth 2011; Lockwood and Porcelli 2013), and finds lower levels of output quantity and quality in Wales than England, when controlling for expenditure. In terms of distributive efficiency, the sheer take-up of school breakfasts and free swimming imply that positive distributional effects are likely (Bolton and Martin 2012; Hopkins 2012). Longer-term gains in dynamic efficiency appear less promising however, as the Welsh government has chosen to protect revenue rather than capital expenditure in response to UK government budget cuts (Drakeford 2012). To date, there has been no systematic research addressing the question of allocative efficiency, but survey data suggest that citizens in Wales are more satisfied with their public services than those in England (Andrews and Martin 2007). The size of the Yes vote in the 2010 referendum on the devolution of further powers when compared to that in the 1997 referendum on devolution *per se*, also implies that Welsh voters are pleased with the devolution dividend.

Broadly speaking, the evidence from the NDC evaluations suggests that there have been improvements in most outcomes relative to comparator areas not benefiting from the NDC, which implies that distributive efficiency has improved (Lawless 2011). This is something that has also emerged from independent analysis of employment data for NDC areas (Gutierrez-Romero 2009). Other research indicates that participation in NDC projects was inclusive of different social groups (Beebeejaun and Grimshaw 2011), though inter-group conflict occurred in some areas (Dargan 2009). Wilson's (2012) shadow pricing analysis suggests that improvements in residents' quality of life have also been productively efficient insofar as the monetized benefits of the scheme outweigh its costs. Since the investment in human capital in NDC areas has been relatively successful (Department of Communities and Local Government 2010), dynamic efficiency seems to be unharmed. Even so, with the continuation of projects largely dependent upon NDC funding, the prospect of NDC neighbourhoods becoming self-sustaining still seems remote. In terms of the overall allocative efficiency of the programme, citizen satisfaction grew for some services (e.g. schools and health) but was static for others (e.g. housing) (Foden *et al.* 2010). This highlights that area-based initiatives may be especially prone to uneven results.

To date, much of the research into the impact of PFIs has been anecdotal or case-based, rather than drawing upon the kind of measures and methods that we advocated in previous chapters. For the goal of dynamic efficiency, existing work indicates that PFIs have proven to be a particularly effective means for 'getting things done', with numerous infrastructure projects having occurred that would not otherwise have been the case. Within the UK healthcare sector, the new facilities have also been shown to play a critical role in delivering improved service quality (KPMG 2010). However, questions remain about the costs of achieving these gains in dynamic and productive efficiency, especially the complexities in designing and managing long-term contracts, the affordability of the repayments for public organizations and the risk that continues to be borne by them (Lonsdale 2005). In the UK, the Metronet scheme, that was intended to refresh the London Underground infrastructure, was declared bankrupt due to cost overruns and brought under public ownership by the UK government to the tune of £2 billion (Jupe 2009). Similar examples abound in the NHS (Pollock and Price 2012). In terms of allocative efficiency, research suggests that public service professionals have appreciated the new facilities (Demirag and Khadaroo 2010). However, there are also cases of PFIs being used to build schools in England that were subsequently shut due to lack of demand (Gilligan 2011). Overall then, the efficiency picture for PFIs is very mixed.

Conclusion

In this chapter we have sought to highlight the careful attention policy-makers and public managers should pay to the intertwining of the different dimensions of efficiency. We have argued that this requires that they be frank about the likely impacts of new initiatives on each dimension of efficiency, and that they consider the ways in which differential efficiency impacts can be justified to the citizenry. All of which again underlines the need for rigorous programme evaluation, and that the accounts that policy-makers and public managers give of their work are deeply connected to the notion of public reason.

To meet the demands of public reason, policy-makers and public officials must indicate how and in what ways the varying balance between productive, distributive, dynamic and allocative efficiency is in the public interest. Efforts to accomplish this will probably reflect a fragile compromise between carefully negotiated political priorities and a sound understanding of the limits and possibilities of different policy interventions. Our efficiency case studies indicate that interventions designed to improve allocative or distributive efficiency could result in improvements on other dimensions of efficiency, or, at least, that such interventions are more compatible with such positive externalities. However, interventions aimed at improving the cost-profile of the public sector appear to be more fraught with unintended effects. Our cases suggest that obsessive attention to productive or dynamic efficiency has much more potential to upset the balance between all the different dimensions of efficiency, a danger which is likely to be heightened during periods of fiscal stress. The role of public reason as a regulative ideal to which policies would be held to account is therefore never more important than when proposals for short or long-term savings are being tabled.

8   Conclusion

Efficiency has been rather badly treated in public management research and writing. With a few notable exceptions, it has tended to be defined narrowly and dismissed rapidly. Much of the literature has focused on maximizing outputs over inputs, without asking whether those outputs are the right ones; whether they are being distributed to the right people; and whether, in the long run, they better equip our society and economy for future prosperity and happiness. We hope that this book will make a start in correcting the balance of inquiry. A more broadly defined notion of public service efficiency – which does justice to the four faces we have described – should be centre stage in debates about how and why we are governed.

We do not claim that these are new ideas. All four dimensions have been coined, and in some cases vigorously researched by others, albeit sometimes under different guises. There are good reasons to think that politicians and public managers too, are attuned to the four dimensions of efficiency. The day-to-day management of public services requires practitioners to juggle the priorities implicit in our four dimensions. We do claim though, that these issues have not been brought together in this way before. It is our determination to raise the awareness of the different faces, and explore the relationship between them, that prompted us to write this book.

This concluding chapter does three things: it reviews the arguments developed over the preceding chapters, identifying, where we can, the greater conclusions emerging from them, before then going on to consider some of the further work we think is needed.

Review

The parlous state of debates about public service efficiency is due to some considerable extent to the disconnect between the academic disciplines of economics and politics. The former has developed an elaborate theoretical analysis of efficiency which provides a glowing prospectus for free markets but a dismal prognosis for services provided by the state. While the forces of demand and supply promise efficiency in free markets, they suggest that public services will inevitably be characterized by dysfunction and inefficiency.

The defence of the state's role – largely developed on the margins of economics and in other disciplines like politics and social policy – stands on two legs. First, it is argued that market imperfections necessitate state intervention, and second that state efficiency will be ensured not by demand and supply, but by political institutions – democracy and bureaucracy most prominent among them – which will protect and advance the public interest.

Unfortunately, that is where the debate has stayed with both sides encamped in their respective positions and precious little dialogue between them. The notion of Pareto efficiency – with its requirement that interventions must deliver welfare improvement without individual welfare loss – epitomizes the problem. For economists, Pareto provides the keystone for any analysis of efficiency; for those focused on social and welfare policy, Pareto really is no help at all. The consequence of this dialogue of the deaf has been that work on the efficiency of the state has tended to go one of two ways. A lot of it – predominantly conducted by economists – has analysed the productive efficiency of specific public services like schools and hospitals with increasing methodological sophistication. Everyone else has run away from the efficiency problem altogether. Very often, of course, the efficiency émigrés have continued to study issues closely related to the efficiency problem, as we have defined it, but they have tended to label their work in other ways while complaining bitterly of the dysfunctional effects of obsessive bean counting.

There are, of course, important exceptions to these tendencies. Scholars working on the determinants of satisfaction with, and trust in, government have pointed to important implications for the allocative efficiency of public resources. After decades of reforms focused on improving performance measurement and management, it is chastening to learn that citizens might care more about processes of government – in terms of the who and how of decision-making – than they do the provision of narrowly defined outputs. Similarly, work focused on growth theory and sustainability engages closely with the issue of dynamic efficiency asking what sorts of investments should we be making today to advance the kind of society we want tomorrow. Largely, however, public management has been distrustful of, or even hostile to, efficiency questions regarding them as part of a neo-liberal plot to roll-back, or privatize, the frontiers of the state. We have argued that the efficiency ground does not need to be so narrowly defined and disciplinarily pure as this conventional treatment suggests.

In marked contrast to our other faces, productive efficiency has received a considerable amount of attention in the literature. Its treatment, however, has been rather narrow. While there are large numbers of methodologically innovative studies carried out in a range of different sectors, much of the work has been focused on measuring efficiency almost as an end in itself. We know remarkably little about the relative performance of the various managerial or structural approaches adopted by governments to improve efficiency, although there is increasing evidence that competition, at least in some respects, can drive some improvements in performance. Much of the policy-running, however, has been made by management fads – from merger to LEAN – which lack any evidence base in rigorous empirical work. There are also problems in the measurement of outputs, which can rarely be taken for granted in public management. Built on sometimes questionable assumptions, it is not always clear that the efficiency snapshots, in which the literature abounds, are as reliable as their methodological sophistication would suggest. Kennis and Provan (2009: 442) warn that:

> It is both easy and tempting to measure something (for example, number of clients served) and label it 'performance', and then to rate and rank organizations on the measure and publicize the rankings so that the measure becomes synonymous with performance in people's minds. It is far more difficult to first answer the question, 'what is performance?' and, then, to answer the question, 'how should performance be measured?'

While it has long been acknowledged that governments intervene on the grounds of equity, economists treat these interventions as trade-offs with efficiency. Redistribution either directly through the tax and benefit system, or indirectly through the provision of public services, is seen as inevitably distorting the efficient working of the free market (Stiglitz 2000). While some economists dismiss this as a purely 'political question that can be answered only at the ballot box' (Samuelson and Nordhaus 2005: 39), it is of course core business to every public manager who makes judgements about who gets what services. We argue that the scale of re-distributive effort makes it crucial that we analyse the efficiency of these different interventions. Should governments pursue their distributive agenda through taxes and transfers, targeted initiatives or training, best practice and standards? As we suggest in chapter four, very little work has been done on answering these questions.

Dynamic efficiency again has long been considered by different disciplines under different names. Researchers working in transport, environment and economic growth, to name just a few, have long explored the relative performance of different types of investment in different types of capital. Confusingly, however, the different 'islands of theorizing' (Hooghe and Marks 2003: 234) have developed a baffling array of different mechanisms to address the dynamic efficiency problem. So we have fiscal rules to limit budget deficits; technocratic mechanisms like CBA to improve investment decisions; market-based instruments to correct for missing markets; and voluntary or network approaches which seek to persuade people to just do the right thing. Without claiming that all issues of future versus current consumption can be resolved with the same methodology, there is much common ground across these areas and real opportunities for cross-fertilization between them.

While having received much less attention than the productive dimension and often somewhat hidden away under other headings, work on allocative efficiency has – in surveys, property prices and migration – arrived at strong, although far from straightforward, measures of satisfaction. Equally there is increasing agreement on the types of intervention likely to improve allocative performance. The suggestion that governments need to pay attention to voice, choice and process provides an important counterbalance to exhortations to maximize productive efficiency. Again, however, there is little empirical work on the effectiveness of these interventions or theoretical consideration of whether or how they should be combined. That is to say we do not really know, in practical terms, how these policies should be pursued. Indeed, the relationship between the three subsidiary efficiencies – productive, distributive and dynamic – and the overarching dimension of allocative efficiency is little understood. We do know, however, that improvements in the first three do not necessarily lead to improvements in the last, and that allocative efficiency – as measured by citizen satisfaction – might be compatible, or even consistent with, some inefficiency in the other dimensions.

Although each of our faces of efficiency raises important questions of its own, some of the most important issues raised by this book are considered in chapter seven. An obsessive focus on one dimension of efficiency in isolation from the others is a recipe for the biggest efficiency failure of them all. We have argued that there is absolutely no point in maximizing the efficient production of outputs that are not valued by the citizens. Similarly, expenditures that make no reference to potential distributive or dynamic consequences have the potential to be self-defeating. It follows then that policies need to be designed and evaluated with reference to all four of our dimensions. Simple pressure on particular performance indicators whether inputs or outputs may lead to improvements in productive efficiency, but we need also to consider their broader consequences in terms of distributive, dynamic and allocative efficiency.

Conclusions and questions

Four broader conclusions emerge from this book. The first is that policies or evaluations focused singularly on the productive efficiency of public service production consider only a small part of the picture. While a focus on this face of efficiency may be legitimate in private management, where the other dimensions of efficiency lie outside the firm and can reasonably be expected to manage themselves, in public management, the productive dimension of efficiency is the least important of the four. Public managers are not singularly focused on productive efficiency. Almost every job in public service delivery now carries a set of expectations associated with the distributive, dynamic and allocative dimensions of efficiency. Poor performance in the other three dimensions has the capacity to completely nullify any advantages realized from improvements in productive efficiency. We acknowledge, of course, the practical difficulties of researching all four dimensions at the same time. As we have tried to demonstrate in this book, each dimension hints at weighty issues and wide repercussions. Neither governments nor researchers can be expected to wage war on all four fronts. We do think though that we, as managers and researchers, should be more open in our acknowledgement of these different perspectives and more alive to the broader repercussions of narrowly framed interventions.

Second, alongside the need to diversify away from the productive dimension, we need to deepen our treatment of each of the other dimensions we have considered. As we have written this book we have been painfully conscious of the fact that each chapter is only scraping the surface of the issues considered. All four dimensions – including productive – are empirically complicated and conceptually rich. None of them is easily defined or measured. All four, as we have described them, seem full of potential but thin on detail. They all raise fundamental questions about the purposes and forms of government intervention deserving of much closer study. We have been struck particularly, by the shortage of work evaluating the policies introduced by governments to address particular dimensions. Even in productive efficiency – by far the best researched of our dimensions – little work has been done on the policy interventions presumed to improve productivity. Similarly, while much has been done on equity in its many guises, we could find almost nothing on the relative efficiency of different attempts to improve it.

Third, as we suggested in chapter seven, alongside work on each of the dimensions is the pressing business of understanding the way in which these dimensions interact and respond to different policy stimuli. Although we do not think these issues are new, we do think there is merit in bringing them together and exploring the tensions and opportunities presented by their combination. While it is legitimate to study one dimension of efficiency in isolation from others, a broader evaluation of the merits of particular policies, structures or systems requires some kind of inquiry on all fronts. Again, we know next to nothing about how the different dimensions interact, although we do know that they do not necessarily work in the same direction. We cannot be sure for example that an improvement in productive efficiency will necessarily result in an improvement in satisfaction.

Fourth, we think these issues are particularly important in the current fiscal environment. Indeed as budgets are squeezed by the combined forces of an ageing population and declining or stagnant economies, maximizing the value of scarce public resources has never been more important. We would argue, however, that the balance between the different dimensions of efficiency reflects a fragile compromise between carefully negotiated priorities and a variety of different organizational forms. The extent to which our public services strike an appropriate balance between dimensions is testament to the variety of organizations involved in service delivery. As such, obsessive attention to one dimension of efficiency – or radical changes to organizations or processes – have the potential to upset the balance between different dimensions of efficiency; a danger which is likely to be heightened during periods of fiscal stress, when the pursuit of productive efficiency or even economy without regard to effectiveness, may assume a disproportionate priority.

One face, four faces or more faces?

Finally, we need to ask whether the four faces of efficiency we have discussed are the right ones, or the only ones, we should be considering. While we have questioned their relative importance, productive, dynamic and allocative senses of the term are well established in the literature. Our notion of distributive efficiency is, however, rather more difficult. Conventional economic approaches present equity as antithetical to efficiency and best considered as a trade-off rather than a component part of a greater economic efficiency (Stiglitz 2000). We have argued, however, that an awful lot of government activity is redistributive in its intent. It is also clearly the case that there are a number of different ways of bringing about the improvements in equity that governments want. Our idea of distributive efficiency captures the relative efficiency of these different programmes in terms of tax revenues spent relative to equity improvement delivered. We recognize, however, that this might be a controversial idea in certain quarters.

There are a number of hints through this book that the four faces are not necessarily as distinctive as our treatment of them suggests. As we discussed in chapter seven, broadly defined outcomes like happiness or wellbeing make for some shades of grey in the distinctions between different efficiencies. Thus all four of our dimensions can claim, to some extent, to be focused on translating the input of taxation revenues into the final outcome of improved citizen happiness or wellbeing. Rather than four efficiencies, perhaps we have just one – allocative efficiency – which reports on satisfaction with the tax-service package and the extent to which it makes people happy. But even if we started with a presumption that there is only one dimension of efficiency, we would soon need to reinvent the different dimensions to capture the ways in which governments try to achieve their goals. Producing services, investing in capital and redistributing resources are distinctive enough to merit their own measurement and evaluation.

But if it is helpful to distinguish between the different ways in which governments intervene in the economy and society, perhaps it would be more helpful to have more than four dimensions. While in one sense the universe of efficiencies is almost limitless, we only had a handful of alternative conceptions of efficiency on our long list of contenders for inclusion in the book. Three candidates – discussed or at least hinted at in the literature – are worth mentioning in dispatches.

The idea of *territorial efficiency* explores the match of functions to different levels of government. As we have seen, the benefits of scale should mean that larger governments will enjoy a productive efficiency advantage over smaller governments. Smaller governments, however, should enjoy an allocative advantage over larger governments in that they are closer to their populations and better able to match their preferences. An efficient allocation of functions to different levels of government will then balance, as Schakel (2010: 331) puts it, the 'heterogeneity of preferences on the one hand and interjurisdictional spillovers on the other'. Territorial efficiency suggests that 'Public goods having merely local externalities and local economies of scale are usually provided by persons living in the locality, rather than by central government' (Hooghe and Marks 2009: 237–38). Services requiring a greater scale, and promising broader and more diffuse benefits, lend themselves to central provision. Whether the devolution and decentralization reforms adopted by a number of European governments in the recent past have taken us closer or further away from territorial efficiency is an interesting question. Doerner and Ihlanfeldt (2011) suggest that as well as responding to the adequacy of the tax-service package, property prices also tell us about the appropriateness of different structures of government.

An analysis of *democratic efficiency* would address the relationship between the costs of democratic systems and the outputs or outcomes of government. We pay for these systems on the presumption that democratic participation of some form will communicate our preferences and protect our interests through oversight and scrutiny. More representation should therefore lead to better government. This might not be the case however. Auriol and Gary-Bobo (2012) warn of diminishing returns where too many representatives might translate into corruption and red tape. Bradbury and Crain (2001: 322) find evidence of a 'positive relationship between legislative size and spending across countries, but the effect is far greater in unicameral legislatures than in bicameral legislatures'. Alongside simple counts of representatives there is then scope for work on the relative efficiency of electoral systems, different types of legislature and different varieties of direct democracy. Democratic efficiency may then be framed in terms of the extent to which these different institutional arrangements generate a sense of happiness or subjective well-being amongst citizens. As we suggested in chapter six, some research suggests that direct democracy in its various guises is positively correlated with satisfaction. Frey and Stutzer (2000: 159) suggest that federalism should be added to the list, concluding that, 'direct democracy and federalism are two such institutions systematically affecting individual well-being'. It is perhaps not a surprising irony that governments have been quicker to search for improvement in the efficiency of public service delivery than to pursue the question of democratic efficiency.

Finally, we considered the merits of what might be dubbed *policy efficiency*. The idea stems from the fact that productive efficiency is in many ways a rather old-fashioned way of viewing the business of government. While it is true that governments do still produce goods and services in a bid to achieve their policy ends, this mode of bureaucratic service delivery is of decreasing significance. Governments can adopt a number of different instruments to pursue their ends – from hierarchies to markets, networks and nudges – many of which involve minimal service production in the traditional sense of the word. In such a way, the outcome of a more-educated population could be advanced through the adoption of a number of different instruments. Governments could – as is currently the practice – use the hierarchical mode to employ teachers in state schools and legally require parents to educate their children. Alternatively, they could simply issue vouchers as a subsidy for private provision or even try to persuade parents and communities to assume responsibility for the education of their children on a voluntary or cooperative basis. Finally, governments could develop a series of nudges (Thaler and Sunstein 2009) which would prompt parents and children, as individuals, to make the right choices about their education. The calculation of which of these inputs achieves the best outcome and at what cost would give us a measure of policy efficiency.

Of course, all three of these alternative faces of efficiency coincide to some degree with the more-established dimensions we have discussed. Whether they, and perhaps other dimensions besides, would provide a better framework for the analysis of efficiency of the state is another question.

References

Aaberge, R., Bhuller, M., Langorgen, A. and Mogstad, M. (2010) 'The distributional impact of public services when needs differ', *Journal of Public Economics*, 94(9–10): 549–62.

Abel, A.B., Gregory, N., Lawrence, M., Summers, H. and Zeckhauser, R.J. (1989) 'Assessing dynamic efficiency: Theory and evidence', *The Review of Economic Studies*, 56(1): 1–19.

Ackerman, B. (1980) *Social Justice in the Liberal State*. New Haven, CT: Yale University Press.

Adler, P.S. and Kwon, S.W. (2002) 'Social capital: Prospects for a new concept', *Academy of Management Review*, 27(1): 17–40.

Agasisti, T. and Johnes, G. (2010) 'Heterogeneity and the evaluation of efficiency: The case of Italian universities', *Applied Economics*, 42(11): 1365–75.

Alan, S., Crossley, T.F., Grootendorst, P.V. and Veall, M.R. (2005) 'Distributional effects of "general population" prescription drug programs in Canada', *Canadian Journal of Economics*, 38(1): 128–48.

Alexandre, H. and Charreaux, G. (2004) 'Efficiency of French privatizations: A dynamic vision', *Journal of Corporate Finance*, 10(3): 467–94.

Alford, J. (2009) *Engaging Public Sector Clients: From Service Delivery to Coproduction*. Basingstoke: Palgrave.

Amirkhanyan, A.A. (2008) 'Privatizing public nursing homes: examining the effects on quality and access', *Public Administration Review*, 68(4): 665–80.

Amirkhanyan, A.A., Kim, A.H.J. and Lambright, K.T. (2008) 'Does the public sector outperform the nonprofit and for-profit sectors? Evidence from a national panel study on nursing home quality and access', *Journal of Policy Analysis and Management*, (27)2: 326–53.

Anderson, C. and Guillory, C. (1997) 'Political institutions and satisfaction with democracy: A cross-national analysis of consensus and majoritarian systems', *American Political Science Review*, 91(1): 66–81.

Anderson, L.M., Shinn, C., Fullilove, M.T., Scrimshaw, S.T., Fielding, J.E., Normand, J. and Carandekulis, V.G. (2003) 'The effectiveness of early childhood development programs: A systematic review', *American Journal of Preventive Medicine*, 24(3): 32–46.

Andrews, R. (2010) 'New public management and the search for efficiency', in T. Christensen and P. Laegrid (eds), *The Ashgate Research Companion to New Public Management*. Farnham: Ashgate Press.

——(2013) 'Local government consolidation and financial sustainability: Evidence from England', *Paper Presented at the International Research Symposium on Public Management XVI, Prague.*

Andrews, R. and Entwistle, T. (2010) 'Does cross-sectoral partnership deliver: an empirical exploration of public service effectiveness, efficiency and equity', *Journal of Public Administration Research and Theory*, 20(3): 679–701.

Andrews, R. and Martin, S. (2007) 'Has devolution improved public services? An analysis of the comparative performance of local public services in England and Wales', *Public Money & Management*, 27(2): 149–56.

——(2010) 'Regional variations in public service outcomes: the impact of policy divergence in England, Scotland and Wales', *Regional Studies*, 44(8): 919–34.

Andrews, R. and Van de Walle, S. (2013) 'New Public Management and citizens' perceptions of efficiency, responsiveness, equity and effectiveness', *Public Management Review.*

Andrews, R., Boyne, G.A. and Walker, R.M. (2006) 'Objective and subjective measures of performance: An empirical exploration', in G.A. Boyne, K.J. Meier, L.J. O'Toole and R.M. Walker (eds), *Determinants of Performance in Public Organizations.* Cambridge: Cambridge University Press.

——(2011) 'Dimensions of publicness and organizational performance: a review of the evidence', *Journal of Public Administration Research and Theory*, 21(3): 301–19.

Andrews, R., Boyne, G., Law, J. and Walker, R. (2005) 'External constraints on local service standards', *Public Administration*, 83(3): 639–56.

Annema, J.A., Koopmans, C. and Van Wee, B. (2007) 'Evaluating transport infrastructure investments: The Dutch experience with a standardized approach', *Transport Reviews*, 27(2): 125–50.

Arocena, P. and Oliveros, D. (2012) 'The efficiency of state-owned and privatized firms: Does ownership make a difference?', *International Journal of Production Economics*, 140(1): 457–65.

Arrow, K., Bolin, B., Costanza, R., Dasgupta, P., Folke, C., Holling, C.S., Jansson, B-O., Levin, S., Maler, K-G., Perrings, C. and Pimentel, D. (1995) 'Economic growth, carrying capacity, and the environment', *Science*, 268: 520–21.

Arrow, K.J. and Debreu, G. (1954) 'Existence of a competitive equilibrium for a competitive economy', *Econometrica*, 22(3): 265–90.

Arts, W. and Gelisson, J. (2001) 'Welfare states, solidarity and justice principles: Does the type really matter?' *Acta Sociologica*, 44(4): 283–99.

Aschauer, D.A. (1989) 'Public investment and productivity growth in the group of seven', *Economic Perspectives*, 13(5): 17–25.

Ashworth, R., Boyne, G., and Entwistle, T. (eds) (2010) *Public Service Improvement: Theories and Evidence.* Oxford: Oxford University Press.

Ashworth, R. and Entwistle, T. (2010) 'The contingent relationship between public management reform and public service work', in P. Blyton, E. Heery and P. Turnbull (eds), *Reassessing the Employment Relationship.* Basingstoke: Palgrave.

Atkinson, A., Burgess, S., Croxson, B., Gregg, P., Propper, C., Slater, H. and Wilson, D. (2009) 'Evaluating the impact of performance-related pay for teachers in England', *Journal of Labour Economics*, 16(3): 251–61.

Atkinson, T. (2005) *Atkinson Review: Final Report, Measurement of Government Output and Productivity for the National Accounts.* Basingstoke: Palgrave.

Aucoin, P. (1990) 'Administrative reform in public management: Paradigms, principles, paradoxes and pendulums', *Governance*, 3(2): 115–37.

Audit Commission (2012) *Striking a Balance: Improving Councils' Decision-making on Reserves*. London: Audit Commission.

Auerbach, A.J., Gokhale, J. and Kotlikoff, L.J. (1994) 'Generational accounting: A meaningful way to evaluate fiscal policy', *Journal of Economic Perspectives*, 8(1): 73–94.

Auriol, E. and Gary-Bobo, R.J. (2012) 'On the optimal number of representatives', *Public Choice*, 153(3–4): 419–45.

Bailey, S.J., Asenova, D. and Hood, J. (2010) 'An exploratory study of the utilisation of the UK's prudential borrowing framework', *Public Policy and Administration*, 25(4): 347–63.

Baker, S. and White, P. (2010) 'Impacts of free concessionary travel: Case study of an English rural region', *Transport Policy*, 17(1): 20–26.

Baldwin, R. (2008) 'Regulation lite: The rise of emission trading', *Regulation and Governance*, 2(2): 193–215.

Banzhaf, S. and Walsh, R. (2008) 'Do people vote with their feet? An empirical test of Tiebout's mechanism', *The American Economic Review*, 98(3): 843–63.

Barratt, E. (2009) 'Governing public servants', *Management and Organizational History*, 4(1): 67–84.

Barrell, R. and Weale, M. (2010) 'Fiscal policy, fairness between generations, and national saving', *Oxford Review of Economic Policy*, 26(1): 87–116.

Barrilleaux, C., and Davis, B. (2003) 'Explaining state-level variations in levels and change in the distribution of income in the United States, 1978–90', *American Politics Research*, 31(3): 280–300.

Barro, R.J. (1991) 'Economic growth in a cross section of countries', *The Quarterly Journal of Economics*, 106(2): 407–43.

——(2001) 'Human capital and growth', *The American Economic Review*, 91(2): 12–17.

Barro, R.J. and Lee, J-W. (2010) 'A new data set of educational attainment in the world, 1950–2010', *NBER Working Paper 15902*. Cambridge, MA: National Bureau of Economic Research.

Bates, L. and Santerre, R. (2006) 'Leviathan in the crosshairs', *Public Choice*, 127(1): 133–45.

Beck Jørgensen, T. and Anderson, L. (2011) 'An aftermath of NPM: Regained relevance of public values and public service motivation', in T. Christensen and P. Laegreid (eds), *The Ashgate Research Companion to New Public Management*. Farnham: Ashgate.

Beebeejaun, Y. and Grimshaw, L. (2011) 'Is the "New Deal for Communities" a new deal for equality? Getting women on board in neighbourhood governance', *Urban Studies*, 48(10): 1997–2011.

Bel, G. (2013) 'Local government size and efficiency in capital intensive services: What evidence is there of economies of scale, density and scope?', in S. Lago-Penas and J. Martinez-Vazquez (eds), *The Challenge of Local Government Size: Theoretical Perspectives, International Experience and Policy Reform*. Cheltenham: Edward Elgar.

Bel, G., Fageda, X. and Warner, M.E. (2010) 'Is private production of public services cheaper than public production? A meta-regression analysis of solid waste and water services', *Journal of Policy Analysis and Management*, 29(3): 553–77.

Bell, S., Hindmoor, A. and Mols, F. (2010) 'Persuasion as governance: A state-centric, relational perspective', *Public Administration*, 88(3): 851–70.

Berman, E.M. (1997) 'Dealing with cynical citizens', *Public Administration Review*, 57(2): 105–12.

Bilbao-Osorio, B. and Rodríguez-Pose, A. (2004) 'From R&D to innovation and economic growth in the EU', *Growth and Change*, 35(4): 434–55.

Billis, D. and Glennerster, H. (1998) 'Human services and the voluntary sector: Towards a theory of comparative advantage', *Journal of Social Policy*, 27(1): 79–98.

Bilodeau, N., Laurin, C. and Vining, A. (2007) 'Choice of organizational form makes a real difference. The impact of corporatization on government agencies in Canada', *Journal of Public Administration Research and Theory*, 17(1): 119–47.

Bjørnskov, C., Dreher, A. and Fischer, J. (2008) 'On decentralization and life satisfaction', *Economics Letters*, 99(1): 147–51.

Bjørnskov, C., Dreher, A. and Fischer, J. (2010) 'Formal institutions and subjective well-being: Revisiting the cross-country evidence', *European Journal of Political Economy*, 26(4): 419–30.

Bloom, D.E., Canning, D. and Sevilla, J. (2004) 'The effect of health on economic growth: A production function approach', *World Development*, 32(1): 1–13.

Boardman, C., Bozeman, B. and Ponomariov, B. (2010) 'Private sector imprinting: An examination of the impacts of private sector job experience on public managers' work attitudes', *Public Administration Review*, 70(1): 50–59.

Boex, J. and Martinez-Vazquez, J. (2005) 'The determinants of the incidence of inter-governmental grants: A survey of the international experience', *Andrew Young School of Policy Studies*, Working Paper 06–52.

Bohman, J. (1999) 'Citizenship and norms of publicity: Wide public reason in cosmopolitan societies', *Political Theory*, 27(2): 176–202.

Bohn, H. and Inman, R.P. (1996) 'Balanced-budget rules and public deficits: Evidence from the U.S. states', *Carnegie-Rochester Conference Series on Public Policy*, 45: 13–76.

Bolton, N. and Martin, S. (2012) 'The policy and politics of free swimming', *International Journal of Sport Policy and Politics*. DOI: 10.1080/19406940.2012.656689.

Borge, L-E., Falch, T. and Tovmo, P. (2008) 'Public sector efficiency: The roles of political and budgetary institutions, fiscal capacity and democratic participation', *Public Choice*, 136: 475–95.

Boschken, H.L. (2000) 'Behavior of urban public authorities operating in competitive markets – policy outcomes in mass transit', *Administration & Society*, 31(6): 726–58.

Bouckaert, G. and Van de Walle, S. (2003) 'Comparing measures of citizen trust and user satisfaction as indicators of "good governance"', *International Review of Administrative Sciences*, 69(3): 329–43.

Bowling, A. (1996) 'Healthcare rationing: The public's debate', *British Medical Journal*, 312(7032): 670–74.

Boyle, R. (2006) 'Measuring public sector productivity: Lessons from international experience', *CMPR Discussion Paper*, Dublin: Institute of Public Administration.

Boyne, G.A. (1996) 'Scale, performance and the New Public Management: An empirical analysis of local authority services', *Journal of Management Studies*, 33(6): 809–26.

——(1998) 'Bureaucratic theory meets reality: Public choice and service contracting in US local government', *Public Administration Review*, 58(6): 474–84.

——(2002a) 'Public and private management: What's the difference?', *Journal of Management Studies*, 39(1): 97–122.

——(2002b) 'Concepts and indicators of local authority performance: An evaluation of the statutory frameworks in England and Wales', *Public Money & Management*, 22(2): 17–24.

——(2003) 'What is public service improvement?', *Public Administration*, 81(2): 211–27.

——(2010a) 'Performance management: Does it work?', in G.A. Boyne, G. Brewer and R.M. Walker (eds), *Public Management Performance: Research Directions* Cambridge: Cambridge University Press.

——(2010b) 'Strategic planning', in R. Ashworth, G.A. Boyne and T. Entwistle (eds), *Public Service Improvement: Theories and Evidence*, Oxford: Oxford University Press.

Boyne, G.A. and Chen, A. (2006) 'Performance targets and public service improvement', *Journal of Public Administration Research and Theory*, 17(3): 455–77.

Boyne, G.A., Gould-Williams, J., Law, J. and Walker, R.M. (2002) 'Best Value – Total Quality Management for local government', *Public Money & Management*, 22(3): 9–16.

Bozeman, B. (1993) 'A theory of government "red tape"', *Journal of Public Administration Research and Theory*, 3(3): 273–303.

Bradbury, J. (2003) 'The political dynamics of sub-state regionalisation: A neo-functionalist perspective and the case of decentralisation in the UK', *British Journal of Politics and International Relations*, 5: 543–75.

——(2005) 'Devolution: between governance and territorial politics', *Parliamentary Affairs*, 58(2): 287–302.

Bradbury, J. and Crain, W.M. (2001) 'Legislative organization and government spending: cross-country evidence', *Journal of Public Economics*, 82(3): 309–25.

Bradley, S., Johnes, G. and Millington, J. (2001) 'The effect of competition on the efficiency of secondary schools in England', *European Journal of Operational Research*, 135(3): 545–68.

Brand, F. (2009) 'Critical natural capital revisited: Ecological resilience and sustainable development', *Ecological Economics*, 68(3): 605–12.

Brewer, G. (2003) 'Building social capital: Civic attitudes and behavior of public servants', *Journal of Public Administration Research and Theory*, 13(1): 5–26.

Brueckner, J.K. (1982) 'A test for allocative efficiency in the local public sector', *Journal Public Economics*, 19(3): 311–31.

Brunner, E.J., Cho, S-W. and Reback, R. (2012) 'Mobility, housing markets, and schools: Estimating the effects of inter-district choice programs', *Journal of Public Economics*, 96(7–8): 604–14.

Bryson, J. (2010) 'The future of public and nonprofit strategic planning in the United States', *Public Administration Review*, 70(S1): S255–67.

Buchanan, J.M. (1965) 'An economic theory of clubs', *Economica*, 32(125): 1–14.

Bulkeley, H. and Gregson, N. (2009) 'Crossing the threshold: Municipal waste policy and household waste generation', *Environment and Planning A*, 41(10): 929–45.

Burgess, S., Wilson, D. and Worth, J. (2011) 'A natural experiment in school accountability: the impact of school performance information on pupil progress and sorting', *Centre for Markets and Public Organization*, Working Paper, Bristol: Bristol University.

Cabeza García, L. and Gómez Ansón, S. (2007) 'The Spanish privatisation process: Implications on the performance of divested firms', *International Review of Financial Analysis*, 16(4): 390–409.

Cabinet Office (2008) *Promoting Equality, Valuing Diversity. A Strategy for the Civil Service.* London: Cabinet Office.

Cammann, C. (1976) 'Effects of the use of control systems', *Accounting, Organizations and Society*, 1(4): 301–14.

Campbell, J.L. and Pedersen, O.K. (2007) 'The varieties of capitalism and hybrid success: Denmark in the global economy', *Comparative Political Studies*, 40(3): 307–32.

Caplow, T. (1954) *The Sociology of Work*. Minneapolis, MN: University of Minnesota Press.

Carpenter, J. (2006) 'Addressing Europe's urban challenges: Lessons from the EU URBAN community initiative', *Urban Studies*, 43(12): 2145–62.

Carr-Saunders, A.M. and Wilson, A. (1933) *The Professions*. Oxford: Clarendon.

Casey, T. (2004) 'Social capital and regional economies in Britain', *Political Studies*, 52(1): 96–117.

Causa, O. and Chapuis, C. (2010) 'Equity in student achievement across OECD countries: An investigation of the role of policies', *OECD Journal: Economic Studies*, Paris: OECD.

Choi, S. (2009) 'Diversity in the U.S. federal government: Diversity management and employee turnover in federal agencies', *Journal of Public Administration Research and Theory*, 19(3): 603–30.

Clark, T., Elsby, M. and Love, S. (2002) 'Trends in British public investment', *Fiscal Studies*, 23(3): 305–42.

Clifton, J., Diaz-Fuentes, D., Fernandez-Gutierrez, M., James, O., Jilke, S. and Van de Walle, S. (2013) *Satisfaction, Voice and Choice in European Public Services*, COCOPS.

Coase, R. (1937) 'The nature of the firm', *Economica*, 4(16): 386–405.

Colegrave, A.D. and Giles, M.J. (2008) 'School cost functions: A meta-regression analysis', *Economics of Education Review*, 27(6): 688–96.

Cooke, P., Gomez, U.M. and Etxebarria, G. (1997) 'Regional innovation systems: Institutional and organisational dimensions', *Research Policy*, 26(4–5): 475–91.

Cowell, R., Downe, J., Martin, S. and Chen, A. (2012) 'Public confidence and public services: It matters what you measure', *Policy and Politics*, 40(1): 120–40.

Crampton, F. (2009) 'Spending on school infra-structure: Does money matter', *Journal of Educational Administration*, 47(3): 305–22.

Crewson, P. (1997) 'Public-service motivation: Building empirical evidence of incidence and effect', *Journal of Public Administration Research and Theory*, 7(4): 499–518.

Daly, H.E. (1992) 'Allocation, distribution, and scale: Towards an economics that is efficient, just, and sustainable', *Ecological Economics*, 6(3): 185–93.

——(1994) 'Operationalising sustainable development by investing in natural capital', in A.M. Jansson, M. Hammer, C. Folke and R. Costanza (eds) *Investing in Natural Capital: The Ecological Economics Approach to Sustainability*, Washington DC: Island Press.

Dargan, L. (2009) 'Participation and local urban regeneration: The case of the New Deal for Communities (NDC) in the UK', *Regional Studies*, 43(2): 305–17.

Darton, R., Forder, J., Netten, A., Bebbington, A., Holder, J. and Towers, A-M. (2010) 'Slicing up the pie: the allocation of central government funding of care for older people', *Social Policy and Administration*, 44(5): 529–53.

Dasgupta, P. and David, P.A. (1994) 'Towards a new economics of science', *Research Policy*, 23(5): 487–521.

Davies, S. (2010) 'Fragmented management, hospital contract cleaning and infection control', *Policy & Politics*, 38(3): 445–63.

De Hoog, R.H., Lowery, D. and Lyons, W.E. (1990) 'Citizen satisfaction with local governance: A test of individual, jurisdictional, and city-specific explanations', *Journal of Politics*, 52(3): 807–37.

De Sa, J. and Lock, K. (2008) 'Will European agricultural policy for school fruit and vegetables improve public health? A review of school fruit and vegetable programmes', *European Journal of Public Health*, 18(6): 558–68.

De Soto, J.H. (2009) *The Theory of Dynamic Efficiency*. Abingdon: Routledge.

De Witte, K. and Geys, B. (2013) 'Citizen coproduction and efficient public good provision: Theory and evidence from public libraries', *European Journal of Operational Research*, 224(3): 592–602.

Deller, S.C. and Chicoine, D.L. (1993) 'Representative versus direct democracy: A test of allocative efficiency in local government expenditures', *Public Finance Review*, 21(1): 100–114.

Deller, S.C. and Maher, C. (2009) 'Government, effectiveness, performance and local property values', *International Journal of Public Administration*, 32(13): 1182–1212.

Demirag, I. and Khadaroo, I. (2010) 'Costs, outputs and outcomes in school PFI contracts and the significance of project size', *Public Money & Management*, 30(1): 13–18.

Denhardt, J.V. and Denhardt, R.B. (2011) *The New Public Service: Serving, not Steering*, 3rd edn. New York: M.E. Sharpe.

Denhardt, R.B. (2004) *Theories of Public Organization*, 4th edn. CA: Wadsworth/ Thomson.

Department of Communities and Local Government (2010) *Improving Outcomes for People in Deprived Neighbourhoods: Evidence from the New Deal for Communities Programme*. London: HMSO.

Diewert, W.E. (2011) 'Measuring productivity in the public sector: Some conceptual problems', *Journal of Productivity Analysis*, 36(2): 177–91.

Dilulio, J.D. (1994) 'Principled agents: The cultural bases of behavior in a federal government bureaucracy', *Journal of Public Administration Research and Theory*, 4(3): 277–318.

Dodgson, M., Hughes, A., Foster, J. and Metcalfe, S. (2011) 'Systems thinking market failure and the development of innovation policy: The case of Australia', *Research Policy*, 40(9): 1145–56.

Doerner, W.M. and Ihlanfeldt, K.R. (2011) 'City government structure: Are some institutions undersupplied?', *Public Choice*, 149(1–2): 109–32.

Dollery, B., Grant, B. and Kortt, M. (2012) *Councils in Cooperation: Shared Services and Australian Local Government*. Sydney: Federation Press.

Domberger, S. and Jensen, P. (1997) 'Contracting out by the public sector: Theory, evidence and prospects', *Oxford Review of Economic Policy*, 13(4): 67–78.

Dowding, K. and John, P. (2008) 'The three exit, three voice and loyalty framework: A test with survey data on local services', *Political Studies*, 56(2): 288–311.

——(2009) 'The value of choice in public policy', *Public Administration*, 87(2): 219–33.

Dowding, K. and Mergoupis, T. (2003) 'Fragmentation, fiscal mobility, and efficiency', *Journal of Politics*, 65(4): 1190–1207.

Downs, A. (1957) *An Economic Theory of Democracy*. New York: Harper.

——(1966) *Inside Bureaucracy*. Boston, MA: Little Brown and Company.

Downs, G.W. and Larkey, P.D. (1986) *The Search for Government Efficiency: From Hubris to Helplessness*. New York: Random House.

Doyle, J.J. (2007) 'Can't buy me love? Subsidizing care of related children', *Journal of Public Economics*, 91(1–2): 281–304.

Drakeford, M. (2012) 'Wales in the age of austerity', *Critical Social Policy*, 32(3): 454–66.

Dranove, D. and Lindrooth, R. (2003) 'Hospital consolidation and costs: Another look at the evidence', *Journal of Health Economics*, 22(6): 983–97.

Du Gay, P. (2000) *In Praise of Bureaucracy: Weber-Organization-Ethics*. London: Sage.

——(2008) '"Without affection or enthusiasm": Problems of involvement and attachment in "responsive public management"', *Organization*, 15(3): 335–53.

Dunleavy, P. (1991) *Democracy, Bureaucracy and Public Choice.* Hemel Hempstead: Harvester Wheatsheaf.

Dunleavy, P. Margetts, H., Bastow, S. and Tinkler, J. (2006) 'New public management is dead – long live digital-era governance', *Journal of Public Administration Research and Theory,* 16(3): 467–94.

Easton, D. (1965) *A Systems Analysis of Political Life.* New York: Wiley.

Eliassen, K.A. and Sitter, N. (2008) *Understanding Public Management.* London: Sage.

Eliasson, J. and Lundberg, M. (2012) 'Do cost–benefit analyses influence transport investment decisions? Experiences from the Swedish transport investment plan 2010–21', *Transport Reviews,* 32(1): 29–48.

Emrouznejad, A., Parker, B.R. and Tavares, G. (2008) 'Evaluation of research in efficiency and productivity: A survey and analysis of the first 30 years of scholarly literature in DEA', *Socio-Economic Planning Sciences,* 42(3): 151–57.

England, R.W. (2000) 'Natural capital and the theory of economic growth', *Ecological Economics,* 34(3): 425–31.

Entwistle, T. (2005) 'Why are local authorities reluctant to externalise (and do they have good reason)?', *Environment and Planning C,* 23(2): 191–206.

Entwistle, T. and Enticott, G. (2007) 'Who or what sets the agenda? The case of rural issues in England's local public service agreements', *Policy Studies,* 28(3): 193–208.

Evandrou, M., Falkingham, J., Hills, J. and Le Grand, J. (1993) 'Welfare benefits in kind and income distribution', *Fiscal Studies,* 14(1): 57–76.

Evans, M. (1999) 'Is public justification central to liberalism?', *Journal of Political Ideologies,* 4(1): 117–36.

Evetts, J. (2003) 'The sociological analysis of professionalism', *International Sociology,* 18(2): 395–415.

Eyles, J., Birch, S., Chambers, S., Hurley, J. and Hutchison, B. (1991) 'A needs-based methodology for allocating health resources in Ontario, Canada: development and an application', *Social Science & Medicine,* 33(4): 489–500.

Fack, G. and Grenet, J. (2010) 'When do better schools raise housing prices? Evidence from Paris public and private schools', *Journal of Public Economics,* 94(1–2): 59–77.

Farrell, D. and McAllister, I. (2006) 'Voter satisfaction and electoral systems: Does preferential voting in candidate-centred systems make a difference?', *European Journal of Political Research,* 45(5): 723–49.

Farrell, M.J. (1957) 'The measurement of productive efficiency', *Journal of the Royal Statistical Society,* 120(3): 253–90.

Farrington, D.P. and Welsh, B.C. (2008) *Saving Children from a Life of Crime.* Oxford: Oxford University Press.

Faulk, D. and Hicks, M. (2011) *Local Government Consolidation in the United States.* Amherst, NY: Cambria Press.

Favell, A. (2001) *Philosophies of Integration: Immigration and the Idea of Citizenship in France and Britain,* 2nd edn. Basingstoke: Palgrave.

Feigenbaum, H., Henig, J.R. and Hamnett, C. (1998) *Shrinking the State: The Political Underpinnings of Privatization.* Cambridge: Cambridge University Press.

Feld, L.P. (1997) 'Exit, voice and income taxes: The loyalty of voters', *European Journal of Political Economy,* 13(3): 455–78.

Feld, L.P. and Matsusaka, J.G. (2003) 'Budget referendums and government spending: evidence from Swiss cantons', *Journal of Public Economics,* 87(12): 2703–24.

Ferrari, A. (2006) 'The internal market and hospital efficiency: A stochastic distance function approach', *Applied Economics,* 38(18): 2121–30.

Foden, M., Grimsley, M., Lawless, P. and Wilson, I. (2010) 'Linking interventions to outcomes in area regeneration: The New Deal for Communities programme in England', *Town Planning Review*, 81(2): 151–71.

Francois, P. (2000) 'Public service motivation as an argument for government provision', *Journal of Public Economics*, 78(3): 275–99.

Frankel, J. and Schreger, J. (2013) 'Over-optimistic official forecasts and fiscal rules in the Eurozone', *Review of World Economics*, 149(2): 247–72.

Freund, E.A. and Morris, I.L. (2005) 'The lottery and income inequality in the States', *Social Science Quarterly*, 86(S1): 996–1012.

Frey, B.S. and Stutzer, A. (2000) 'Maximizing happiness', *German Economic Review*, 1(2): 145–67.

Fries, J.F., Koop, C.E., Beadle, C.E., Cooper, P.P., England, M.J., Greaves, R.F., Sokolov, J.J. and Wright, D. (1993) 'Reducing health care costs by reducing the need and demand for medical services', *The New England Journal of Medicine*, 329(5): 321–25.

Fukuyama, F. (2001) 'Social capital, civil society and development', *Third World Quarterly*, 22(1): 7–20.

Fung, A. and Wright, E. (2001) 'Deepening democracy: Innovations in empowered participatory governance', *Politics and Society*, 29(1): 5–41.

Furmana, J.L., Porter, M.E. and Stern, S. (2002) 'The determinants of national innovative capacity', *Research Policy*, 31(6): 899–933.

Gaffney, D., Pollock, A., Price, D. and Shaoul, J. (1999) 'PFI in the NHS – Is there an economic case?', *British Medical Journal*, 319(7202): 116–19.

Gajduschek, G. (2003) 'Bureaucracy: Is it efficient? Is it not? Is that the question? Uncertainty reduction: An ignored element of bureaucratic rationality', *Administration and Society*, 34(6): 700–723.

Gay, G. (2007) 'The rhetoric and reality of NCLB', *Race, Ethnicity and Education*, 10(3): 279–93.

Gaynor, M., Moreno-Serra, R. and Propper, C. (2010) 'Death by market power: reform, competition and patient outcomes in the National Health Service', *NBER Working Paper 16164*.

Gemmill, M.C., Thomson, S. and Mossialos, E. (2008) 'What impact do prescription charges have on efficiency and equity? Evidence from high income countries', *International Journal for Equity in Health*, 7(12): 1–22.

Gerdtham, U-G., Lothgren, M., Tambour, M. and Rehnberg, C. (1999) 'Internal markets and health care efficiency: A multiple output Stochastic Frontier Analysis', *Health Economics*, 8(1): 151–64.

Gershon, P. (2004) *Releasing Resources to the Front-line: Independent Review of Public Sector Efficiency*. London: HMSO.

Gill, N. and Rodriguez-Pose, A. (2012) 'Do citizens really shop between decentralised jurisdictions? Tiebout and internal migration revisited', *Space and Polity*, 16(2): 175–95.

Gilligan, A. (2011) 'PFI: £70m bill for schools that had to close', *The Telegraph*, 26th January.

Gonzalez, M.M. and Trujillo, L. (2008) 'Reforms and infrastructure efficiency in Spain's container ports', *Transportation Research Part A*, 42(1): 243–57.

Goodsell, T. (1983) *The Case for Bureaucracy: A Public Administration Polemic*. Chatham, NJ: Chatham House Publishers, Inc.,

Gordon, N. and Knight, B. (2008) 'The effects of school district consolidation on educational cost and quality', *Public Finance Review*, 36(4): 408–30.

Gramlich, E.M. (1994) 'Infrastructure investment: A review essay', *Journal of Economic Literature*, 32(3): 1176–96.

Grandy, C. (2009) 'The "efficient" public administrator: Pareto and a well-rounded approach to public administration', *Public Administration Review*, 69(6): 1115–23.

Gray, J. (2000) *Two Faces of Liberalism*. Oxford: Polity Press.

Greenaway, J. (2004) 'Celebrating Northcote/Trevelyan: Dispelling the myths', *Public Policy and Administration*, 19(1): 1–14.

Greenwald, B. and Stiglitz, J.E. (1986) 'Externalities in economies with imperfect information and incomplete markets', *Quarterly Journal of Economics*, 101(2): 229–64.

Greve, C. and Hodge, G. (2010) 'A transformative perspective on public private partnerships', in T. Christensen and P. Laegrid (eds) *The Ashgate Research Companion to New Public Management*. Farnham: Ashgate.

Grimes, M. (2006) 'Organizing consent: The role of procedural fairness in political trust and compliance', *European Journal of Political Research*, 45(2): 285–315.

Groeneveld, S. and Verbeek, S. (2012) 'Diversity policies in public and private sector organizations: An empirical comparison of incidence and effectiveness', *Review of Public Personnel Administration*, 32(4): 353–81.

Grosskopf, S. and Yaisawamg, S. (1990) 'Economies of scope in the provision of local public services', *National Tax Journal*, 43(1): 61–74.

Grossman, G.M. and Helpman, E. (1990) 'Trade, innovation and growth', *American Economic Review*, 80(2): 86–91.

Gulick, L. (1937) 'Science, values and public administration', in L. Gulick and L. Urwick (eds) *Papers on the Science of Administration*. New York: Columbia University.

Gulick, L. and Urwick, L. (eds) (1937) *Papers on the Science of Administration*. New York: Columbia University.

Gutierrez Romero, R. (2009) 'Estimating the impact of England's area-based intervention "New Deal for Communities" on employment', *Regional Science and Economics*, 39 (3): 323–31.

Gutmann, A. and Thompson, D. (1996) *Democracy and Disagreement*. Cambridge, MA: Harvard University Press.

Haas-Wilson, D. and Garmon, C. (2011) 'Hospital mergers and competitive effects: Two retrospective analyses', *International Journal of the Economics of Business*, 19(1): 17–32.

Hansen, M.B. (2010) 'Marketization and economic performance: Competitive tendering in the social sector', *Public Management Review*, 12(2): 255–74.

Hanushek, E.A. (1989) 'The impact of differential expenditures on school performance', *Educational Researcher*, 18(4): 45–62.

—— (1997) 'Assessing the effects of school resources on student performance: An update', *Education Evaluation and Policy Analysis*, 19(2): 141–64.

Hanushek, E.A. and Woessmann, L. (2011) 'How much do educational outcomes matter in OECD countries?', *Economic Policy*, 26(67): 427–91.

Harrow, J. (2002) 'New Public Management and social justice: Just efficiency or equity as well?', in K. McLaughlin, S.P. Osborne and E. Ferlie (eds) *New Public Management: Current Trends and Future Prospects*. London: Routledge.

Hart, J.A. and Cowhey, P.F. (1977) 'Theories of collective goods re-examined', *Western Political Quarterly*, 30(3): 351–62.

Hayes, K.J., Razzolini, L. and Ross, L.B. (1998) 'Bureaucratic choice and nonoptimal provision of public goods: Theory and evidence', *Public Choice*, 94(1–2): 1–20.

Heal, G. (2012) 'Defining and measuring sustainability', *Review of Environmental Economics and Policy*, 6(1): 147–63.

Heald, D. and Dowdall, A. (1999) 'Capital charging as a VFM tool in public services', *Financial Accountability & Management*, 15(3): 229–47.

Hedley, T.P. (1998) 'Measuring public sector effectiveness: Using private sector methods', *Public Productivity & Management Review*, 21(3): 251–58.

Hefetz, A. and Warner, M. (2004) 'Privatization and its reverse: Explaining the dynamics of the government contracting process', *Journal of Public Administration Research and Theory*, 14(2): 171–90.

Herian, M.N., Hamm, J.A, Tomkins, A.J. and Pytlik Zillig, L.M. (2012) 'Public participation, procedural fairness, and evaluations of local governance: The moderating role of uncertainty', *Journal of Public Administration Research and Theory*, 22(4): 815–40.

Hibbing, J. and Theiss-Morse, E. (2001) 'Process preferences and American politics: What the people want government to be', *American Political Science Review*, 95(1): 145–53.

Hicks, J.R. (1939) 'The foundations of welfare economics', *Economic Journal*, 49(196): 696–712.

Hilber, C., Lyytikäinen, T. and Vermeulen, W. (2011) 'Capitalization of central government grants into local house prices: Panel data evidence from England', *Regional Science and Urban Economics*, 41(4): 394–406.

Hilber, C.A.L. and Mayer, C.J. (2009) 'Why do households without children support local public schools? Linking house price capitalization to school spending,' *Journal of Urban Economics*, 65(1): 74–90.

Hills, J. (2002) 'Following or leading public opinion: Social security policy and public attitudes since 1997', *Fiscal Studies*, 23(4): 539–58.

Hindricks, J. and Myles, G.D. (2006) *Intermediate Public Economics*. Cambridge, MA: MIT Press.

Hirschman, A.O. (1970) *Exit, Voice and Loyalty: Responses to Declines in Firms, Organizations and States*. Cambridge, MA: Harvard University Press.

Hodge, G. (1998) 'Contracting public services: A meta-analytic perspective of the international evidence', *Australian Journal of Public Administration*, 57(4): 98–110.

Hodge, G.A. (2000) *Privatization: An International Review of Performance*. Boulder, CO: Westview Press.

Hodge, G. and Greve, C. (2007) 'Public–Private Partnerships: an international performance review', *Public Administration Review*, 67(3): 545–58.

Hoffmann, V. (2007) 'EU ETS and investment decisions: The case of the German electricity industry', *European Management Journal*, 25(6): 464–74.

Hoggett, P. (1991) 'A new management in the public sector', *Policy and Politics*, 19(4): 243–56.

——(2006) 'Conflict, ambivalence, and the contested purpose of public organizations', *Human Relations*, 59(2): 175–94.

Hood, C. (1990) 'Public administration: lost an empire, not yet found a role', in A. Leftwich (ed.) *New Developments in Political* Science. Aldershot: Edward Elgar.

——(1991) 'A public management for all seasons', *Public Administration*, 69(1): 3–19.

Hood, J., Fraser, I. and McGarvey, N. (2006) 'Transparency of risk and reward in UK public–private partnerships', *Public Budgeting & Finance*, 26(4): 40–58.

Hood, J., Aseniova, D., Bailey, S and Manochin, M. (2007) 'The UK's prudential borrowing framework: A retrograde step in managing risk?', *Journal of Risk Research*, 10(1): 49–66.

Hooghe, L. and Marks, G. (2003) 'Unraveling the central state, but how? Types of multi-level governance', *American Political Science Review*, 97(2): 233–43.

——(2009) 'Does efficiency shape the territorial shape of government', *Annual Review of Political Science*, 12(1): 225–41.

Hopkins, J. (2012) 'How Wales led the way on school breakfast clubs', *The Observer*, Sunday 16th September.

Hoynes, H.W., Scanzenbach, D.W. and Almond, D. (2012) 'Long run impacts of childhood impact to the safety net', *NBER Working Paper 18535*.

Hugh-Jones, D. (forthcoming) 'Why do crises go to waste? Fiscal austerity and public service reform', *Public Choice*.

Iversen, T. (2005) *Capitalism, Democracy and Welfare*. Cambridge: Cambridge University Press.

Jacob, B.A. (2004) 'Public housing, housing vouchers, and student achievement: Evidence from public housing demolitions in Chicago', *American Economic Review*, 94(1): 233–258.

James, O. (2011a) 'Managing citizens' expectations of public service performance: Evidence from observation and experimentation in local government', *Public Administration*, 89(4): 1419–35.

——(2011b) 'Performance measures and democracy: Information effects on citizens in field and laboratory experiments', *Journal of Public Administration Research and Theory*, 21(3): 399–418.

James, O. and John, P. (2007) 'Public management at the ballot box: Performance information and electoral support for incumbent English local governments', *Journal of Public Administration Research and Theory*, 17(4): 567–80.

Jensen, A. and Stelling, P. (2007) 'Economic impacts of Swedish railway deregulation: A longitudinal study', *Transportation Research Part E – Logistics and Transportation Review*, 43(5): 516–34.

Jilke, S. and Van de Walle, S. (2012) 'Two track public services?', *Public Management Review*, DOI:10.1080/14719037.2012.664015..

John, P., Dowding, K. and Biggs, S. (1995) 'Residential mobility in London: A micro-level test of the behavioural assumptions of the Tiebout model', *British Journal of Political Science*, 25(3): 379–97.

Johnson, G.E., Scholes, K. and Whittington, R. (2008) *Exploring Corporate Strategy*, 8th edn. London: Prentice Hall.

Julius, D. (2008) *Public Services Industry Review. Understanding the Public Services Industry: How Big, How Good, Where Next?* London: Department for Business, Enterprise and Regulatory Reform.

Jupe, R. (2009) 'New Labour, public–private partnerships and rail transport policy', *Economic Affairs*, 29(1): 20–25.

Kaldor, N. (1939) 'Welfare propositions in economics and interpersonal comparisons of utility', *Economic Journal*, 49(145): 549–52.

Kao, G. and Thompson, J.S. (2003) 'Racial and ethnic stratification in educational achievement and attainment', *Annual Review of Sociology*, 29: 417–42.

Kaplan, R.S. and Norton, D.P. (1996) *The Balanced Scorecard: Translating Strategy into Action*. Boston, MA: Harvard Business School Press.

Kavanagh, D. (1985) 'Whatever happened to consensus politics?', *Political Studies*, 33(4): 529–46.

Keating, M. (1998) *The New Regionalism in Western Europe: The State and Political Authority in the Major Democracies*. Northampton: Edward Elgar.

Kelly, J.M. and Swindell, D. (2002) 'Service quality variation across urban space: First steps toward a model of citizen satisfaction', *Journal of Urban Affairs*, 24(3): 271–88.

Kelman, S. and Friedman, J.N. (2009) 'Performance improvement and performance dysfunction: An empirical examination of distortionary impacts of the emergency room wait-time target in the English National Health Service', *Journal of Public Administration Research and Theory*, 19(4): 917–46.

Kennis, K. and Provan, K.G. (2009) 'Towards an exogenous theory of public network effectiveness', *Public Administration*, 87(3): 440–56.

Kingsley, D.J. (1945) 'Political ends and administrative means: The administrative principles of Hamilton and Jefferson', *Public Administration Review*, 5(1): 87–89.

Kisby, B. (2010) 'The big society: Power to the people?', *Political Quarterly*, 81(4): 484–91.

Kling, J.R., Liebman, J.B. and Katz, L.E. (2007) 'Experimental analysis of neighbourhood effects', *Econometrica*, 75(1): 83–119.

Knack, S. and Keefer, P. (1997) 'Does social capital have an economic pay off?', *Quarterly Journal of Economics*, 112(4): 1251–88.

Knapp, M., Hallam, A., Beecham, J. and Baines, B. (1999) 'Private, voluntary or public? Comparative cost-effectiveness in community mental health care', *Policy and Politics*, 27(1): 25–41.

Knudsen, E.I., Heckman, J.J., Cameron, J.L. and Shonkoff, J.P. (2006) 'Economic, neurobiological and behavior perspectives on building America's future workforce', *Proceedings of the National Academy of Sciences*, 103: 10155–62.

KPMG (2010) *Operating Healthcare Infrastructure: Analysing the Evidence*. London: KPMG.

Kraak, S.B.M., Bailey, N., Cardinale, M., Darby, C., DeOliveira, J.A.A., Eero, M., Graham, N., Holmes, S., Jakobsen, T., Kempf, A., Kirkegaard, E., Powell, J., Scott, R. D., Simmonds, E.J, Ulrich, C., Vanhee, W. and Vinther, M. (2012) 'Lessons for fisheries management from the EU cod recovery plan', *Marine Policy*, 37: 200–213.

Kuntz, L. and Vera, A. (2007) 'Modular organization and hospital performance', *Health Services Management Review*, 20(1): 48–58.

Landefeld, J.S., Seskin E.P. and Fraumeni, B.M. (2008) 'Taking the pulse of the economy: Measuring GDP', *The Journal of Economic Perspectives*, 22(2): 193–216.

Laslier, J-F. and Picard, N. (2002) 'Distributive politics and electoral competition', *Journal of Economic Theory*, 103(1): 106–30.

Lawless, P. (2011) 'Understanding the scale and nature of outcome change in area-regeneration programmes: Evidence from the New Deal for Communities programme in England', *Environment and Planning C*, 29(3): 520–32.

Lax, D.A. and Sebenius, J.K. (1987) *The Manager as Negotiator*. New York: Free Press.

Lax, J. and Phillips, J. (2012) 'The democratic deficit in the state', *American Journal of Political Science*, 56(1): 148–66.

Layard, R. (2006) 'Happiness and public policy: A challenge to the profession', *The Economic Journal*, 116(510): 24–33.

Le Grand, J. (1997) 'Knights, knaves or pawns? Human behaviour and social policy', *Journal of Social Policy*, 26(2): 149–69.

——(2006) 'Equality and choice in public services', *Social Research*, 73(2): 695–710.

Lee, K.S., Chun, K.H. and Lee, J.S. (2008) 'Reforming the hospital service structure to improve efficiency: urban hospital specialization', *Health Policy*, 87(1): 41–49.

Lerner, A.P. (1944) *The Economics of Control*. New York: Macmillan.

Levin, H.M. (1998) 'Educational vouchers: Effectiveness, choice and costs', *Journal of Policy Analysis and Management*, 17(3): 373–92.

Lewis, D.R. and Dundar, H. (1999) 'Costs and productivity in higher education: theory, evidence and policy implications', in J.C. Smart and W.G. Tierney (eds) *Higher Education: Handbook of Theory and Research*, 14. Springer.

Lijphart, A. (1999) *Patterns of Democracy: Government forms and performance in thirty-six countries*. New Haven, CT: Yale University Press.

Lindblom, C. (1959) 'The science of muddling through', *Public Administration Review*, 19(2): 79–88.

Ling, T. (2002) 'Delivering joined-up government in the UK: Dimensions, issues and problems', *Public Administration*, 80(4): 615–42.

Lipsky, M. (1980) *Street-level Bureaucracy: Dilemmas of the Individual in Public Services*. New York: Russell Sage.

Lockwood, B. and Porcelli, F. (2013) 'Incentive schemes for local government', *CESIfo DICE Report*, 11(1): 55–63.

Lomax, K.S. (1943) 'Expenditure per head and size of population', *Journal of the Royal Statistical Society*, 106(1): 51–59.

——(1952) 'A criterion of efficiency in local administration', *Journal of the Royal Statistical Society*, 115(4): 521–23.

Lonsdale, C. (2005) 'Post-contractual lock-in and the UK Private Finance Initiative (PFI): the cases of national savings and investments and the Lord Chancellor's departments', *Public Administration*, 83(1): 67–88.

Lorenzen, M. (2007) 'Social capital and localised learning: Proximity and place in technological and institutional dynamics, *Urban Studies*, 44(4): 799–817.

Lowndes, V., Pratchett, L. and Stoker, G. (2001) 'Trends in public participation: citizens' perspectives', *Public Administration*, 79(2): 445–55.

Lukes, S. (1974) *Power: A Radical View*. New York: Macmillan.

Lundvall, B. (2007) 'National innovation systems – Analytical concept and development tool', *Industry and Innovation*, 14(1): 95–119.

Lynn, L.E. (2006) *Public Management: Old and New*. London: Routledge.

MacDonald, D.V. (1999) 'Applying the concept of natural capital criticality to regional resource management', *Ecological Economics*, 29(1): 73–87.

Macinati, M.S. (2008) 'The relationship between quality management systems and organizational performance in the Italian National Health Service', *Health Policy*, 85(2): 228–41.

Mackie, J. and Preston, J.M. (1998) 'Twenty-one sources of error and bias in transport project appraisal', *Transport Policy*, 5(1): 1–7.

Margolis, M. (1979) *Viable Democracy*. New York: St Martin's Press.

Matsusaka, J.G. (1995) 'Fiscal effects of the voter initiative: Evidence from the last 30 years', *Journal of Political Economy*, 103(3): 587–623.

——(2005) 'Direct democracy works', *Journal of Economic Perspectives*, 19(2): 185–206.

——(2010) 'Popular control of public policy: A quantitative approach', *Quarterly Journal of Political Science*, 5(2): 133–67.

Maynard-Moody, S. and Musheno, M. (2000) 'State agent or citizen agent: Two narratives of discretion', *Journal of Public Administration Research and Theory*, 10(2): 329–58.

McAdam, R. and Walker, T. (2003) 'An inquiry into balanced scorecards within Best Value implementation in UK local government', *Public Administration*, 81(4): 873–92.

MacNaughton, A., Matthews, T. and Pittman, J. (1998) '"Stealth tax rates": Effective versus statutory marginal tax rates', *Canadian Tax Journal*, 46(5): 1029–66.

Mercier Ythier, J. (2010) 'Regular distributive efficiency and the distributive liberal social contract', *Journal of Public Economic Theory*, 12(5): 943–78.

Merton, R.K. (1940) 'Bureaucratic structure and personality', *Social Forces*, 18(4): 560–68.

Middleton, P. (ed.) (2010) *Delivering Public Services that Work*. Axminster: Triarchy Press.

Mintzberg, H. (2004) *Managers not MBAs: A Hard Look at the Soft Practice of Managing and Management Development*. San Francisco, CA: Berrett-Koehler Publishers.

Mitchell, G. (2005) 'Forecasting environmental equity: Air quality responses to road user charging in Leeds, UK', *Journal of Environmental Management*, 77(3): 212–26.

Mittnik, S. and Neumann, T. (2001) 'Dynamic effects of public investment: Vector autoregressive evidence from six industrialised countries', *Empirical Economics*, 26(2): 429–46.

Moene, K.O. and Wallerstein, M. (2003) 'Earnings inequality and welfare spending: A disaggregated analysis', *World Politics*, 55(4): 485–516.

Moore, M.H. (1994) 'Public value as the focus of strategy', *Australian Journal of Public Administration*, 53(3): 296–303.

——(1995) *Creating Public Value: Strategic Management in Government*. Cambridge, MA: Harvard University Press.

Morgan, R. (2002) 'Address to the National Policy Centre', Swansea: University of Wales.

Morgeson, F.V. and Petrescu, C. (2011) 'Do they all perform alike? An examination of perceived performance, citizen satisfaction and trust with US federal agencies', *International Review of Administrative Sciences*, 77(3): 451–79.

Mosher, F. (1968) *Democracy and the Public Service*. New York: Oxford University Press.

Moynihan, D. (2013) 'Does public service motivation lead to budget maximization? Evidence from an experiment', *International Public Management Journal*, 16(2): 179–196.

Naff, K.C. and Kellough, J.E. (2003) 'Ensuring employment equity: Are federal diversity programs making a difference?', *Public Administration Review*, 26(12): 1307–36.

National Consumer Council (NCC) (2007) *Delivering Public Services: Service Users' Experience of the Third Sector by the National Consumer Council*. London: NCC.

Neshkova, M. and Guo, H. (2012) 'Public participation and organizational performance: Evidence from State agencies', *Journal Public Administration Research and Theory*, 22(2): 267–88.

Newman, A.L. (2003) 'When opportunity knocks: Economic liberalisation and stealth welfare in the United States', *Journal of Social Policy*, 32(2): 179–97.

Newman, J. and Clarke, J. (2009) *Publics, Politics and Power: Remaking the Public in Public Services*. London: Sage.

Nguyen-Hoang, P. and Yinger, J. (2011) 'The capitalization of school quality into house values: A review', *Journal of Housing Economics*, 20(1): 30–48.

Niskanen, W. (1971) *Bureaucracy and Representative Government*. Chicago, IL: Aldine Atherton.

——(1973) *Bureaucracy: Servant or Master?* London: IEA.

Nordhaus, W.D. and Tobin, J. (1972) 'Is growth obsolete? Economic research: Retrospect and prospect', *Economic Growth*, 5: 1–80.

O'Toole, L.J. and Meier, K.J. (2004a) 'Parkinson's Law and the New Public Management? Contracting determinants and service quality consequences in public education', *Public Administration Review*, 64(3): 342–52.

O'Toole, L.J., Jr. and Meier, K.J. (2004b) 'Desperately seeking Selznick: Co-optation and the dark side of public management in networks', *Public Administration Review*, 64(6): 681–93.

Oates, W.E. (1969) 'The effects of property taxes and local public spending on property values: An empirical study of tax capitalization and the Tiebout hypothesis', *Journal of Political Economy*, 77(6): 957–61.

——(1999) 'An essay on fiscal federalism', *Journal of Economic Literature*, 37(3): 1120–49.

OECD (2010), *PISA 2009 results: What Makes a School Successful? – Resources, Policies and Practices (Volume IV)*. Paris: OECD Publishing.

Office of the Deputy Prime Minister (2003) *Equality and Diversity in Local Government in England: A Literature Review*. London: HMSO.

OFSTED (2013) *The Framework for School Inspection*. Manchester: OFSTED.

Osborne, D. and Gaebler, T. (1992) *Reinventing Government: How the Entrepreneurial Spirit is Transforming the Public Sector*. Reading, MA: Addison Wesley.

Osborne, S. (2006) 'The new public governance?', *Public Management Review*, 8(3): 377–87.

Ostrom, E., Burger, J., Field, C.B., Norgaard, R.B. and Policansky, D. (1999) 'Revisiting the commons: Local lessons, global challenges', *Science, 284(5412): 278–82*.

Pandey, S.K. and Stazyk, E.C. (2008) 'Antecedents and correlates of public service motivation', in J.L. Perry and A. Hondeghem (eds) *Motivation in Public Management*, Oxford: Oxford University Press.

Parker, D. and Hartley, K. (2003) 'Transaction costs, relational contracting and public private partnerships: A case study of UK Defence', *Journal of Purchasing and Supply Management*, 9(3): 97–108.

Parsons, T. (1939) 'The professions and social structure', *Social Forces*, 17(4): 457–67.

Partha, D. and David, P.A. (1994) 'Towards a new economics of science', *Research Policy*, 23(5): 487–521.

Pearce, D.W. and Atkinson, G.D. (1993) 'Capital theory and the measurement of sustainable development: An indicator of "weak" sustainability', *Ecological Economics*, 8(2): 103–8.

Pendleton, A. (1999) 'Ownership or competition? An evaluation of the effects of privatization on industrial relations: institutions, processes and outcomes', *Public Administration*, 77(4): 769–91.

Perkin, H. (1989) *The Rise of Professional Society, England Since 1880*. London and New York: Routledge.

Perry, J.L. (2000) 'Bringing society in: Towards a theory of public service motivation', *Journal of Public Administration Research and Theory*, 10(2): 471–88.

Perry, J.L., Engbers, T.A. and Jun, S.Y. (2009) 'Back to the future? Performance-related pay, empirical research and the perils of persistence', *Public Administration Review*, 69(1): 39–51.

Perry, J.L., Hondeghem, A. and Wise, L.R. (2010) 'Revisiting the motivational bases of public service: Twenty years of research and an agenda for the future', *Public Administration Review*, 70(5): 681–90.

Peters, B.G., Schröter, E. and von Maravic, P. (eds) (2012) *The Politics of Representative Bureaucracy – Power, Legitimacy, Performance*. Cheltenham: Edward Elgar.

Pfeffer, J. and Salancik, G. (1978) *The External Control of Organizations: A Resource Dependence Perspective*. New York: Harper & Row.

Pitts, D.W. and Wise, L.R. (2010) 'Workforce diversity in the new millennium: Prospects for research', *Review of Public Personnel Administration*, 30(1): 44–69.

Pitts, D.W. (2009) 'Diversity management, job satisfaction and performance: Evidence from U.S. federal agencies', *Public Administration Review*, 60(2): 328–38.

Pollitt, C. (1988) 'Bringing consumers into performance measurement concepts: consequences and constraints', *Policy and Politics*, 16(2): 77–87.

Pollitt, C. and Bouckaert, G. (2011) *Public Management Reform: A Comparative Analysis – New Public Management, Governance, and the Neo-Weberian State*. Oxford: Oxford University Press.

Pollock, A. and Price, D. (2012) 'How Libor rate rigging has put hospitals in crisis', *The Guardian*, 20 December.

Pollock, A.M., Price, D. and Player, S. (2007) 'An examination of the UK Treasury's evidence base for cost and time overrun data in UK Value-for-money policy and appraisal', *Public Money & Management*, 27(2): 127–34.

Pressman, J.L. and Wildavsky, A. (1973) *Implementation*. Berkeley, CA: University of California Press.

Prest, A.R. and Turvey, R. (1965) 'Cost-benefit analysis: A survey', *The Economic Journal*, 75(300): 683–35.

Propper, C. (2012) 'Competition, incentives and the English NHS', *Health Economics*, 21(1): 33–40.

Pugh, D.S., Hickson, D.J. and Hinings, C.R. (1971) *Writers on Organizations*. Harmondsworth: Penguin.

Quigley, C. (1966) *Tragedy and Hope: A History of the World in Our Time*. New York: Macmillan.

Quinn, J. (1980) *Strategies for Change: Logical Incrementalism*. Homewood, IL: Richard D. Irwin.

Radnor, Z. (2010) *Review of Business Process Improvement Methodologies in Public Services*. London: Advanced Institute of Management.

Radnor, Z. and Osborne, S. (2013) 'Lean: A failed theory for public services?', *Public Management Review*, 15(2): 265–87.

Rainey, H.G. (1993) 'A theory of goal ambiguity in public organizations', in J.L. Perry (ed.) *Research in Public Administration*, volume 2. Greenwich, CT: JAI Press.

Rainey, H.G. and Steinbauer, P. (1999) 'Galloping elephants: Developing elements of a theory of effective government organizations', *Journal of Public Administration Research and Theory*, 9(1): 1–32.

Rawlings, L.B. and Rubio, G.M. (2005) 'Evaluating the impact of conditional cash transfer programs', *World Bank Research Observer*, 20(1): 29–55.

Rawls, J. (1972) *A Theory of Justice*. London: Oxford University Press.

——(1996) *Political Liberalism*. New York: Columbia University Press.

Raz, J. (1986) *The Morality of Freedom*. Oxford: Oxford University Press.

Reback, R. (2005) 'House prices and the provision of local public services: Capitalization under school choice programs', *Journal of Urban Economics*, 57(2): 275–301.

Reingewertz, Y. (2012) 'Do municipal amalgamations work? Evidence from municipalities in Israel', *Journal of Urban Economics*, 72(2–3): 240–51.

Revelli, F. and Tovmo, P. (2007) 'Revealed yardstick competition: Local government efficiency patterns in Norway', *Journal of Urban Economics*, 62(1): 121–34.

Rhodes, J., Tyler, P. and Brennan, A. (2005) 'Assessing the effect of area based initiatives on local area outcomes: Some thoughts based on the national evaluation of the single regeneration budget in England', *Urban Studies*, 42(11): 1919–46.

Rich, M.J. (1989) 'Distributive politics and the allocation of federal grants', *American Political Science Review*, 83(1): 193–213.

Ritzer, G. (1975) 'Professionalization, bureaucratization and rationalization: The views of Max Weber', *Social Forces*, 53(4): 627–34.

——(1983) 'The McDonaldization of society', *Journal of American Culture*, 6(1): 100–107.

Roch, C.H. and Poister, T.H. (2006) 'Citizens, accountability and service satisfaction: The influence of expectations', *Urban Affairs Review*, 41(3): 292–308.

Rodden, J. (2002) 'The dilemma of fiscal federalism: grants and fiscal performance around the world', *American Journal of Political Science*, 46(3): 670–87.

Rodríguez-Pose, A. and Crescenzi, R. (2008) 'Research and development, spillovers, innovation systems, and the genesis of regional growth in Europe', *Regional Studies*, 42(1): 51–67.

Rodriquez-Pose, A. and Gill, N. (2003) 'The global trend towards devolution and its implications', *Environment and Planning C*, 21(3): 333–51.

Rodríguez Pose, A. and Maslauskaite, A. (2012) 'Can policy make us happier? Individual characteristics, socio-economic factors and life satisfaction in Central and Eastern Europe', *Cambridge Journal of Regions, Economy and Society*, 5(1): 77–96.

Rodriguez-Pose, A., Tijmstra, S.A.R. and Bwire, A. (2009) 'Fiscal decentralisation, efficiency, and growth', *Environment and Planning A*, 41(9): 2041–62.

Roine, J., Vlachos, J. and Waldenstrøm, D. (2009) 'The long-run determinants of inequality: What can we learn from top income data?', *Journal of Public Economics*, 93(7–8): 974–988.

Ruggerio, J. (1996) 'Efficiency of education production: An analysis of New York school districts', *Review of Economics and Statistics*, 78(3): 499–509.

Rutgers, M.R. and van der Meer, H. (2010) 'The origins and restriction of efficiency in public administration: regaining efficiency as the core value of public administration', *Administration & Society*, 42(7): 755–59.

Salmon, P. (1987) 'Decentralisation as an incentive scheme', *Oxford Review of Economic Policy*, 3(2): 24–43.

Salter, A.J. and Martin, B.R. (2001) 'The economic benefits of publicly funded basic research', *Research Policy*, 30(3): 509–32.

Samuelson, P.A. (1954) 'A pure theory of public expenditure', *Review of Economics and Statistics*, 36(4): 387–89.

Samuelson, P.A. and Nordhaus, W.D. (2005) *Economics*, 18th edn. New York: McGraw-Hill.

Santerre, R. (1986) 'Representative versus direct democracy: A Tiebout test of relative performance', *Public Choice*, 48(1): 55–63.

Savas, E.S. (1987) *Privatization: The Key to Better Government*. Chatham, NJ: Chatham House.

Sawyer, M. (2007) 'Fiscal policy under New Labour', *Cambridge Journal of Economics*, 31(6): 885–99.

Schachter, H.L. (2007) 'Does Frederick Taylor's ghost still haunt the halls of government? A look at the concept of governmental efficiency in our time', *Public Administration Review*, 67(5): 800–810.

Schaechter A., Kinda, T., Budina, N. and Weber, A. (2012) 'Fiscal rules in response to the crisis—Toward the "next-Generation" rules. A new dataset', *IMF Working Paper*, WP/12/187.

Schakel, A.H. (2010) 'Explaining regional and local government: An empirical test of the decentralization theorem', *Governance*, 23(2): 331–55.

Schein, V.E. (1979) 'Examining an illusion: The role of deceptive behaviours in organizations', *Human Relations*, 32(4): 287–95.

Schröter, E. and von Maravic, P. (2012) 'The performance claim of representative bureaucracy: can it deliver?', in B.G. Peters, E. Schröter and P. von Maravic (eds) *The Politics of Representative Bureaucracy – Power, Legitimacy, Performance*. Cheltenham: Edward Elgar.

Schubert, T. (2009) 'Empirical observations on New Public Management to increase efficiency in public research – boon or bane?', *Research Policy*, 38(8): 1225–34.

Schuknecht, L., Moutot, P., Rother, P. and Stark, J. (2011) 'The stability and growth pact: Crisis and reform', *ECB Occasional Paper*, No. 129.

Schultz, T.W. (1961) 'Investment in human capital', *The American Economic Review*, 51(1): 1–17.

Schwab, K. (2012) *The Global Competitiveness Report 2012–2013*. Geneva: World Economic Forum.

Seddon, J. (2008) *Systems Thinking in the Public Sector: The Failure of a Reform Regime and a Manifesto for a Better Way*. Axminster: Triarchy Press.

Self, P. (1985) *Political Theories of Modern Government: Its Role and Reform*. London: Allen and Unwin.

Selznick, P. (1966) *TVA and the Grass Roots*, 2nd edn. New York: Harper and Row.

Serra, G. (1995) 'Citizen initiated contact and satisfaction with bureaucracy', *Journal of Public Administration Research and Theory*, 5(2): 175–88.

Shaoul, J., Stafford, A. and Stappleton, P. (2011) 'NHS capital investment and PFI: From central responsibility to local affordability', *Financial Accountability and Management*, 27(1): 1–17.

Sharp, E. (1984) ' "Exit, voice and loyalty" in the context of local government problems', *The Western Political Quarterly*, 37(1): 67–83.

Shepherd, W. (1990) *The Economics of Industrial Organisation*. Englewood Cliffs, NJ: Prentice Hall.

Sidique S.F., Joshi, S.V. and Lupi, F. (2010) 'Factors influencing the rate of recycling: An analysis of Minnesota counties', *Resources, Conservation and Recycling*, 54(4): 242–49.

Simon, H.A. (1944) 'Decision-making and administrative organization', *Public Administration Review*, 4(1): 16–30.

——(1976) *Administrative Behavior: A Study of Decision-making Processes in Administrative Organization*, 3rd edn. London: Macmillan.

Simpson, H. (2009) 'Productivity in public services', *Journal of Economic Surveys*, 23(2): 250–76.

Sirin, S.R. (2005) 'Socio-economic status and academic achievement: A meta-analytic review of research', *Review of Educational Research*, 75(3): 417–53.

Söderlund, N., Csaba, I., Gray, A., Milne, R. and Raftery, J. (1997) 'Impact of the NHS reforms on English hospital productivity: An analysis of the first three years', *British Medical Journal*, 315(7116): 1126–29.

Sowels, N. (2011) 'From prudence to profligacy: How Gordon Brown undermined Britain's public finances', in N. Champroux and C. Coron (eds) *Les Politiques Economiques des Années Brown, 1997–2010*. Observatoire de la Sociétié Britannique.

Spang, H.R., Arnould, R.J. and Bazzoli, G.J. (2009) 'The effect of non-rural hospital mergers and acquisitions: An examination of cost and price outcomes', *The Quarterly Review of Economics and Finance*, 49(2): 323–42.

Spector, M. and Kitsuse, J. (1977) *Constructing Social Problems*. Menlo Park, CA: Cummings.

Stadelmann, D. (2010) 'Which factors capitalize into house prices? A Bayesian averaging approach', *Journal of Housing Economics*, 19(3): 180–204.

Stavins, R.N., Wagner, A.F. and Wagner, G. (2003) 'Interpreting sustainability in economic terms: Dynamic efficiency plus intergenerational equity', *Economics Letters*, 79(3): 339–43.

Stevens, M. (2012) 'The cost-effectiveness of UK parenting programmes for preventing children's behaviour problems – a review of the evidence', *Child & Family Social Work*, DOI: 10.1111/j.1365–2206.2012.00888.x.

Stigler, G. (1958) 'The economics of scale', *Journal of Law and Economics*, 1: 54–71.

Stiglitz, J.E. (2000) *Economics of the Public Sector.* New York: W.W. Norton & Co.

Stipak, B. (1979) 'Citizen satisfaction with urban services: Potential misuse as a performance indicator', *Public Administration Review*, 39(1): 46–52.

——(1980) 'Local governments' use of citizen surveys', *Public Administration Review*, 40(5): 521–25.

Stoker, G. (2006) 'Public value management: A new narrative for networked governance?', *American Review of Public Administration*, 36(1): 41–57.

Studlar, D.T., MacAllister, I. and Ascui, A. (1990) 'Privatization and the British electorate: microeconomic policies, macroeconomic evaluations, and party support', *American Journal of Political Science*, 34(2): 565–98.

Suleiman, E. (2003) *Dismantling Democratic States.* Princeton, NJ: Princeton University Press.

Sullivan, H., Barnes, M. and Matka, E. (2006) 'Collaborative capacity and strategies in area based initiatives', *Public Administration*, 84(2): 289–310.

Swann, D. (1988) *The Retreat of the State: Deregulation and Privatisation in the UK and US.* London: Harvester/Wheatsheaf.

Swider, S.M. (2002) 'Outcome effectiveness of community health workers: An integrative literature review', *Public Health Nursing*, 19(1): 11–20.

Swygert, M.I. and Yanes, K.E. (1998) 'A unified theory of justice: the integration of fairness into efficiency', *Washington Law Review*, 73(2): 249–327.

Taylor, F.W. (1911) *The Principles of Scientific Management.* New York: Harper & Bros.

——(1916) 'Government efficiency', *Bulletin of the Taylor Society*, 2(5): 7–13.

Thaler, R. and Sunstein, C. (2009) *Nudge: Improving Decisions About Health, Wealth and Happiness.* London: Penguin.

Thompson, F. (1987) 'Lumpy goods and cheap riders: An application of the theory of public goods to international alliances', *Journal of Public Policy*, 7(4): 431–49.

Thompson, W. (2002) *Managing Change to Improve Public Services: Top Down or Bottom Up?* London: Office of Public Service Reform.

Tiebout, C. (1956) 'A pure theory of local expenditure', *Journal of Political Economy*, 64(5): 416–24.

Tolbert, C. and Mossberger, K. (2006) 'The effects of e-government on trust and confidence in government', *Public Administration Review*, 66(3): 354–69.

Tullock, G. (1965) *The Politics of Bureaucracy.* Washington DC: Public Affairs Press.

Tyler, T. (1988) 'What is procedural justice: Criteria used by citizens to assess the fairness of legal procedures', *Law and Society Review*, 22(1): 103–36.

Ulbig, S. (2002) 'Policies, procedures, and people: Sources of support for government?', *Social Science Quarterly*, 83(3): 789–809.

Urwick, L. (1937) 'Organization as a technical problem', in L. Gulick and L. Urwick (eds) *Papers on the Science of Administration.* New York: Columbia University Press.

Van Dooren, W., Bouckaert, G. and Halligan, J. (2010) *Performance Management in the Public Sector.* London: Routledge.

Van Ryzin, G. (2007) 'Pieces of a puzzle linking government performance, citizen satisfaction, and trust', *Public Performance & Management Review*, 30(4): 521–35.

——(2011) 'Outcomes, process and trust of civil servants', *Journal of Public Administration, Research and Theory*, 21(4): 745–60.

Van Ryzin, G., Immerwahr, S. and Altman, S. (2008) 'Measuring street cleanliness: A comparison of New York City's scorecard and results from a citizen survey', *Public Administration Review*, 68(2): 295–303.

Vickerman, R. (2007) 'Cost-benefit analysis and large-scale infrastructure projects: State of the art and challenges', *Environment and Planning. C*, 34(4): 598–610.

Victor, A. (1991) 'Indicators of sustainable development: Some lessons from capital theory', *Ecological Economics*, 4(3): 191–213.

Viner, J. (1960) 'The intellectual history of laissez-faire', *Journal of Law and Economics*, 3: 45–69.

Vining, A. and Boardman, A. (1992) 'Ownership versus competition: Efficiency in public enterprise', *Public Choice*, 73(2): 205–39.

Waldo, D. (1948) *The Administrative State: A Study of the Political Theory of American Public Administration*. New York: The Ronald Press Company.

——(1952) 'Development of theory of democratic administration', *American Political Science Review*, 46(1): 81–103.

Walker, H. (1937) *Public Administration in the United States*. New York: Farrar & Reinhart.

Walker, R.M. and Andrews, R. (forthcoming) 'Local government management and performance: A review of the evidence', Working Paper, *Journal of Public Administration Research and Theory*.

Ward, H. and John, P. (1999) 'Targeting benefits for electoral gain: constituency marginality and the distribution of grants to English local authorities', *Political Studies*, 47(1): 32–52.

Warner, M. (2001) 'Building social capital: The role of local government', *Journal of Socio-Economics*, 30(2): 187–92.

Warner, M. and Hefetz, A. (2012) 'Insourcing and outsourcing: the dynamics of privatization among U.S. municipalities, 2002–7', *Journal of the American Planning Association*, 78(3): 313–27.

Weale, A. (2011) 'New modes of governance, political accountability and public reason', *Government and Opposition*, 46(1): 58–80.

Weber, M. (1947) *The Theory of Social and Economic Organization*. New York: Free Press.

Weisbrod, B.A. (1997) 'The future of the non-profit sector: Its entwining with private enterprise and government', *Journal of Policy Analysis and Management*, 16(4): 541–55.

Welsh Assembly Government (2006) *Making the Connection – Delivering Beyond Boundaries*. Cardiff: Welsh Assembly Government.

Westlund, H. and Adam, F. (2010) 'Social capital and economic performance: A meta-analysis of 65 studies', *European Planning Studies*, 18(6): 893–919.

Whitehead, M., Dahlgren, G. and Evans, T. (2001) 'Equity and health sector reforms: Can low-income countries escape the medical poverty trap', *The Lancet*, 358(9284): 833–36.

Wilensky, H.L. (1964) 'The professionalization of everyone?', *American Journal of Sociology*, 70(2): 137–58.

Willetts, D. (2011) *The Pinch: How the Baby Boomers Took Their Children's Future – and Why They Should Give it Back*. London: Atlantic Books.

Williams, D.W. (2003) 'Measuring government in the early Twentieth Century', *Public Administration Review*, 63(6): 643–59.

Williamson, O.E. (1967) 'Hierarchical control and optimum firm size', *Journal of Political Economy*, 75(2): 123–38.

——(1981) 'The economics of organization', *American Journal of Sociology*, 87(3): 548–77.

Wilson, I. (2012) 'Using shadow pricing to value outcomes: Evidence from the New Deal for Communities programme in England', *Town Planning Review*, 83(6): 669–93.

Wilson, J., Tyedmers, P. and Pelot, R. (2007) 'Contrasting and comparing sustainable development indicator metrics', *Ecological Indicators*, 7(2): 299–314.

Wilson, P.A. (1997) 'Building social capital: A learning agenda for the twenty-first century', *Urban Studies*, 34(5–6): 745–60.

Wittman, D. (1989) 'Why democracies produce efficient results', *Journal of Political Economy*, 97(6): 1395–1424.

Woesmann, L. (2007) 'International evidence on school competition, autonomy and accountability', *Peabody Journal of Education*, 82(2–3): 473–97.

Wolf, C. (1987) 'Market and non-market failures: Comparison and assessment', *Journal of Public Policy*, 7(1): 43–70.

Wolff, E. and Zacharias, A. (2007) 'The distributional consequences of government spending and taxation in the U.S., 1989 and 2000', *Review of Income and Wealth*, 53(4): 692–715.

Woolcock, M. (1998) 'Social capital and economic development: Toward a theoretical synthesis and policy framework', *Theory and Society*, 27(2): 151–208.

Woolcock, M. and Narayan, D. (2000) 'Social capital: Implications for development theory, research, and policy', *World Bank Research Observer*, 15(2): 225–49.

Wright, B. (2007) 'Public service and motivation: Does mission matter?', *Public Administration Review*, 67(1): 54–64.

Xu, K.T. (2006) 'State-level variations in income-related inequality in health and health achievement in the U.S.', *Social Science & Medicine*, 63(2): 457–64.

Zhang, Y.-J. and Wei, Yi-M. (2010) 'An overview of current research on EU ETS: Evidence from its operating mechanism and economic effect', *Applied Energy*, 87(6): 1804–14.

Index

Taylor & Francis

eBooks

FOR LIBRARIES

ORDER YOUR
FREE 30 DAY
INSTITUTIONAL
TRIAL TODAY!

Over 23,000 eBook titles in the Humanities, Social Sciences, STM and Law from some of the world's leading imprints.

Choose from a range of subject packages or create your own!

Benefits for **you**

▶ Free MARC records
▶ COUNTER-compliant usage statistics
▶ Flexible purchase and pricing options

Benefits for your **user**

▶ Off-site, anytime access via Athens or referring URL
▶ Print or copy pages or chapters
▶ Full content search
▶ Bookmark, highlight and annotate text
▶ Access to thousands of pages of quality research at the click of a button

For more information, pricing enquiries or to order a free trial, contact your local online sales team.

UK and Rest of World: **online.sales@tandf.co.uk**

US, Canada and Latin America:
e-reference@taylorandfrancis.com

www.ebooksubscriptions.com

ALPSP Award for
BEST eBOOK
PUBLISHER
2009 Finalist

Taylor & Francis eBooks
Taylor & Francis Group

A flexible and dynamic resource for teaching, learning and research.